BAR BOOK

ALSO BY JULIE SHEEHAN

Orient Point

Thaw

To the Readers & Citizens of the
Riverhead Free Library!

BAR BOOK

POEMS AND OTHERWISE

[signature]

JULIE SHEEHAN

W. W. NORTON & COMPANY NEW YORK LONDON

For information about permission to reproduce selections from this book,
write to Permissions, W. W. Norton & Company, Inc.,
500 Fifth Avenue, New York, NY 10110

For information about special discounts for bulk purchases, please contact
W. W. Norton Special Sales at specialsales@wwnorton.com or 800-233-4830

Manufacturing by Courier Westford
Book design by JAM Design
Production manager: Anna Oler

Library of Congress Cataloging-in-Publication Data

Sheehan, Julie.
Bar book : poems and otherwise / Julie Sheehan. — 1st ed.
p. cm.
ISBN 978-0-393-07217-4 (hardcover)
1. Bartenders—Poetry. I.Title.
PS3619.H44B37 2010
811'.6—dc22

2010006110

W. W. Norton & Company, Inc.
500 Fifth Avenue, New York, N.Y. 10110
www.wwnorton.com

W. W. Norton & Company Ltd.
Castle House, 75/76 Wells Street, London W1T 3QT

1 2 3 4 5 6 7 8 9 0

Contents

NIGHT SHIFT

Prosper the work of our hands, O Lord;

prosper the work of our hands.

—Psalm 90

***

LUNCH SHIFT

Brandy Stinger

You young ones wouldn't know where to begin
with all the strappy contraptions trussing up us old birds.
Girdles! Lord, where do you buy those catastrophizing things anymore!
Back then courtships were long, honeybunch; they *had* to be
just to figure out the clothes, not to mention getting them off. Yes,
I'll have one more and that's it. But at least you knew how to dress
then, and which aisle was lingerie and which was men's briefs!
I stopped trying to shop in 1975, when my husband died. Now, child,
it's too confusing. You can't tell a lawyer from a rap star.
Just *look* at the shoes the girls wear! Deadweights! Back in Texas
we used to tie things like those to sacks of doomed puppies, why,
every time I see such shoes I think the poor girl's liable to drown.
Though I do confess, the ones we wore may have been a little unkind,
expecting your foot to assume a triangular formation to which it did not
          naturally incline,
but they got you where you wanted to go: married,
however unstably, but secure, knowing you'd both totter on.
All right one more, and that's final. I don't envy you
your loose fits, your quick change.

A Word About Problem Customers

Remember how your parents would say "Life's not fair"? It's true. Life is a teetering, drunken, upside down pyramid. 5% of the world's population consumes 26% of its energy. 5% of the population in the U.S. holds nearly 70% of its wealth. And 5% of a bar's customers demand 95% of a bartender's time but supply 2% of her income. What props up this crazed geometry? Service. As small galaxies, restaurants perpetuate the great one's lopsidedness with cheerful, unremitting obedience. Obedience, in turn, attracts Problem Customers,[1] whose sole pursuit is to join the sunny side of that 5-to-95% ratio without paying capital gains. In the Problem Customer's mind, restaurants are obliged to provide him an inversion of resources the benefits of which he does not enjoy in the rest of his shabby existence. While life's not fair, you, the service industry professional, must fight this particular injustice, not because you are a principled Marxist (are you?), but because at the end of your shift you need to have amassed enough capital to catch a cab home and pay the sitter.

---

1. The first time I waited on him, he ordered a Suffering Bastard, and another, and another. Then, could he have the grilled vegetables on rice, only as a salad, and with the grain somehow transubstantiated into French fries at no extra cost? Could he? By closing time he was drinking Black Bush and joking that my tip would double if only I'd kiss him. The next day, as I was opening up, he materialized, a Mendicant in a crisp blue oxford. He put his heels together and apologized from a throat deeper than an empty pocket. We married soon after.

Fortunately, you can identify the Problem Customers with almost no luck or skill, and you won't need this quiz unless you are remedial in the basics of the human psyche, which betrays itself with comic speed. Match the item on the left with its correlative on the right.

A steer-built bald-o in his Elks Club blazer jokes about an adverse effect on your tip when he discovers Tête de Boeuf misspelled on the specials list.

Sorry, we're out of that.

Her reading glasses have sighed down her delicate nose and are ready to take a suicidal leap. She holds the menu at arm's length, staving it off because it very well might be about to lick her face. "Don't you have any *freshwater* fish?" She lobs her query over the front of the menu, which says "Reggie's Crystal Beer Parlor."

Let's start with your lovely daughter.

Armani shoulder to Armani shoulder, the two square off against the bar, a Mondrian among Louise Bourgeoises. Their eyes glisten from having just discovered a college acquaintance on the "What's Hot" list in *New York Magazine.* "Do you know how to make . . ." They await your worshipful "no." They've read about it already. "Do you know how to make . . . a Suffering Bastard?"

Would you like that glazed or crusted?

Starve these maws of the labor they would gorge upon. Supply must not follow demand, mutt that it is. Only in cases of endangerment—Mr. Bald-O's tablecloth is afire; Nasal Lady has severed an artery; the hipsters are choking on their cashmere socks—do you rush to serve.

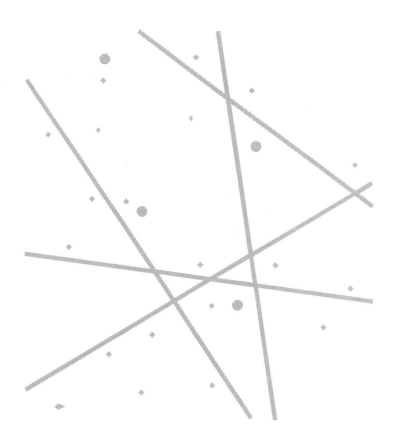

Calling the Banns

(Includes Choice of Bloody Mary or Mimosa)

Hear ye, hear ye, hear ye, dearly beloved who gather:
Step out from behind thy table tents, thy Florentines and Benedicts.
Cease the deadpan crackle of pushed-away plates.
Let it be known that, under this wall sconce, on the day of our Lord
      Too Soon, Just Met,
I call the banns of—hey, listen up, folks, I'm talking here.

      Do you, Barmaid, renounce the House Tab?
      Do you pour contempt, secret sin of butlers, in the thistles out back?
      Do you quench henceforth no others, returning the key
          to the ram's horn hook
      And untie your apron, shake for shake,
      And free a new storyline from its raveling hem?

For when the last customer said, "Swirl thine bitters in this cup,"
      you swirled,
And when the owner said, "Lo! Let us be open," you opened yourself to any.
Then entered here divers Masters, publicans, swine, sinners,
      Whiskey Flips and Strega Sours,
      Juleps, Kirs, Hot Toddies.

And the first to enter was the Dark and Stormy,
      for you were but Goslings both.
And he lamented, "Why do you not let me enter?

For Kristen let Brett enter, and Belinda let Jim."
And you replied, "Wherefore say you Belinda let Jim?
Belinda let not Jim."
But he said, "Belinda let Jim."
And you, "No."
And he, "Yes."
And you, "Why let she Jim?"
And he, "Because he said he loved her."
And he gave you the Goslings rum and said he loved you,
And you, you let him enter.

     And do you, The Usual, amend thy habits?
     Do you seek instead to serve?
     Then forswear the cucumber garnish,
     Forswear the ginger beer, and to the mint sprig,
         say "Begone!"
     Perchance your taste in crockware differs,
         canst thou say unto her "pretty"?
     Canst thou harden not thy heart?

For when you were a boy, you took the topshelf unto yourself,
     the Very Special Old Pale you assumed,
And helped not your sister in the kitchen.

And hours have you tolled in your usual bar,
And hours have you told of your lineage: of your father,
     of your father's father, of your father's father's father,

And the Barmaid listened, filling your glass
     even as you filled her ear,
And the fathers poured forth, and fathers, and fathers,
     and fathers' farther fathers,
And the Barmaid spake at last: "And what,"
     quoth she, "of the mothers?"
And answered you, "Who cares."

If any man do allege and declare
any impediment—

A silence reigneth, six centuries long.

Marge, let's go; *Survivor*'s on in twenty minutes.

Have you no mercy, Harold? Tell them:
You will accuse each other of having changed.
You will hurl suspicions, have a child,
Name her after considerable conflict.
Your insults will lack vigor.
You will be poor, make bad choices
From the *prix fixe* early bird.
You will not forgive, but hate
Will seat you next to each other
In its crowded way.

Matins. Praise God in his sanctuary. Now, while it is empty. Prepare the way: bar mops, beer, garnishes, glasses, ice bins, liquors, mixers, for you do not know the hour. Each shift sings a new song, following demand, that burbling crowd; therefore must your craft anticipate the unpredictable.[2] Today, someone could order a frozen Banana Daiquiri. A dozen other patrons could see the frozen Banana Daiquiri en route to a table and decide they want one as well. At once, the way is frozen Banana Daiquiri. Just as a cryptographer sifts through rapidly shifting probabilities and reassigns priorities until, one after another, letters drop into place or are rejected, Daiquiris go out or bills are settled, the mind of a bartender stays fluid, looking for small resolutions of a demand that will never be satisfied but that will swirl on, like evolution, like virtuosity, revealing its method in practice. *While* is the operative word. Pour the soda back *while* the Ankle Breaker chills. *While* the stout settles, dust the Pilgrim Cocktail with some fresh grated nutmeg. *While* is the rhythm of craft, to which drinks line up by themselves, and once it is going, only a lack of foresight can break it. The artful bartender does not leave a half-formed Nirvana to fetch more tamarind syrup from a crawl space in Ur, because the artful bartender restocked before the church got full.

Lauds. Awaken the barstools from their upside-down sleep.

---

2. Reader, I married him. Reader, we had a child. Reader, we divorced. A predictable trinity. My office now is to locate the precise point where my moral code fractured. Lunch shift. Swing shift. Night shift. If only I can retrace my liturgical formularies, I can find it: the breakdown of craft that accounts for our fall. "Cassis should have been Chartreuse," I could say, instead of the usual evasions: "It ended badly," "We drifted" or "He doesn't love me." Strictly speaking, "Marry-Child-Divorce" deciphers the narrative arc. Still, I am not satisfied. Action has its shadow government, choice, and somewhere is a singular failure I can own. I will find it, and when I do, I will quit this service forever.

Prime. Enter Red, Bishop Suffragan, a master of anecdote and legendary barman,[3] although legend doesn't pay so he's still working for tips. He comes at noon to count the drawer and leaves or is supposed to leave at seven when the swing shift ends. He often sticks around. We all get two drinks' shift pay, plus fifty bucks under the table. It's advisable now and then to take only the cash and leave Red the drinks.

Terce. Labor is the currency of respect. During this postprandial pause, resupply the lines, not for yourself, but for your successor. It's a matter of ethics. You could, for example, stock the bar with just enough to get through your shift, sticking the night guy with one deforested maraschino cherry and eleven red stems sobbing in their unfathomable brine. Such treachery has been known to occur. Remember, though, that respect in our trade is what you do; its currency is labor, not gesture. Ceremony is for customers, who will never thank you for squeezing more lemons, but if you're serious about being human, get to work.

Sext. Don't drink during your shift. Only Red does that. Also, ignore celebrities.

Tom Collins

Vicious is too mild a word, *mon* Gabe.
He shredded you, talked "Every word you write's
a lie including *and* and *the*" type stuff,

---

3. Early in my courtship with disaster, he took me to one of the few high-end gin mills where the bartenders, like Red, know how to make a proper Old Fashioned. How I lied. "I love it," I said. No wonder his aim suffered.

precision tongue-lashing like a pastry chef.
He even called you a bored English major,
yes he did, girlfriend. What did you do

to rile him so?

And I'm like, sweet pea, homeboy,
listen up Queen Mab, you shush your lip
before Gabe rams a fist through those pearly white

fangs of yours. And he's like, "Oooooh, you know
him?" Know him! Mother of Mailer, I'm meeting him
in twenty minutes at the Slaughterhouse.

Anyhow, I thought you ought to hear
the pulp fiction that hack is hailing down
on your fifteen-dollar haircut. Honestly,

why don't you see Marcello? I gave you his card
eons ago. Run, do not walk. Your bangs
are begging for some quality revision.

So that's the poop, it pains me to report.
He's probably still there, still up the street
at Don Iago's, if you care to tango.

None. Don't tolerate tiny aggressions; they fester and enlarge. Say there's a guy down toward the service end who inherited money from his father's shameful pursuits, a socially inadequate last name, and a southern accent that we're pretty sure is fake. Say his elbows are both up on the bar, crowding out his fellow patrons. His sense of entitlement has already kicked in before he can snap his fingers. Trouble is a Gucci blazer. Indulge him not, even when he promises things. Plus it is a violation of restaurant policy and all-around bad idea to fraternize with the customers.[4]

Evensong. Card the usual suspects, the kid who orders a beer in the generic, without an article: "I'll have beer." Not only are underage drinkers bad for your rap sheet—you can be arrested for serving them—but they're no fun to chat with, they tip in silver, not paper, and they take up space.

Compline. We all believe we're irreplaceable, but in my case it's true.[5]

---

4. How could I resist a charmer with credit card debt and a drinking problem, especially when one of his funniest barfly anecdotes involved both: He wakes up one morning bare naked, his memory equally blank. He hadn't managed to get under the covers of his futon bed last night, but there's something in his hand. What is it? It's a wad of American Express receipts, a money trail of this recent binge. He unpeels the bills, one by one. (Telling the story, he acts out this bit of housekeeping.) The sums get higher as he goes, but his signature devolves, as if in time-lapse photography, from its crispy-spiky sober state on the first receipt to a flat line at the heart of the wad, a charge of $1,000. This story used to make me laugh. When he told it.

5. My affianced was the storyteller, whereas I was drawn to formal matters, the rules, the orders. Our first, flirty summer, he tried to employ me as the fabricator I'm not, asking me to pose as an interested buyer in a sting operation he'd set up to prove to himself a former business partner was thieving his intellectual property. "It's an outrage," he'd say. I said little, hoping he'd cast someone else in his drama, which he eventually did.

continued

Though I could mix what passes for a Tom Collins today, I could never have pulled one off back in 1874, when it first gained popularity not as a cocktail, but as a practical joke. To play it took cruel planning. You had to recruit a network of bartenders in advance. You'd also need a friend who was excitable but ultimately forgiving to be the butt of the joke. You'd tell him, "Some bounder name of Tom Collins is down at McSorley's slandering you!" Once you'd gotten him sufficiently primed to duel this fictional personage, you tailed him while he burst into McSorley's demanding to see Tom Collins. At that cue, the bartender would set him up with a drink, say, "Tom Collins? He went thataway," then direct the hapless soul onward to the next stop in his search for honor. Who knows what the bartender served, a flip, a sling, a julep? These days "Tom Collins" gets you gin, sour mix and club soda, honor being in short supply. I would not have been a successful perpetrator of the hoax, but I see now I could have been the bartender. It would have been immoral, but then so are all complicities: laughing at mean jokes, serving alcoholics, napping in wartime. I would have played along, I was that desperate.

Martini

Holidays are roughest: all that cheer, Dexedrine-
        induced dress sizes, the men like bark-hard
Berries sweating the tang of gin.
Hollow parties cackling ice, parties macled with villain-
        ous mutters—
We were hosting one that night! "There's Carolyn!
You're early! Help yourself to, let's see, vodka, rye, whiskey. Oh, and gin.
No, none for me, I'm on the wagon."
        "Good for you, Lucy."
        "Yes. Chin-chin."

(Lost one evening: T-ball trophy, panty hose, some realms, Cardigan
        Welsh Corgi, tennis bracelet, not cheap,
And the brief letter that launched the latest glissando of gin.
Last seen in handbag. Reward. Dame last seen in Marco's, slugging,
But could be anywhere, given
The supervision.)

I like the upstairs best, the guest room with its twin
        bed set for stashing backup bottles—
You can never be too sure when it comes to gin—
But that day every last one, every prismatic firkin
Down to the airplane nips had been confiscated. The nerve! Wynn,
My husband? No! That freeze-dried has-been?
The kids? I wasn't worried. I hid my elixirs with Machiavellian
        stealth.

No one would suspect one tucked in
Next week's frozen turkey, chilling
        nicely in our Sub-Zero.
The body cavity of an 18-pound Butterball equals a fifth of gin.
But only, it happens, when partly thawed. At one degree Fahren-
        heit, turkey contracts,
Trapping the snap and sting within.

I needed a slug just then of lubricious gin.
I raided the freezer to extrude my steady, my linchpin,
        my steeler in times of stress.
It wouldn't budge, wedged like mortal sin
        in the icy heart of my unrepentant bird.
I wrestled for that soul of gin.
I tugged and coaxed, tried olive oil, Crisco, margarine,
Anything to slacken the passage of my sapphirine
        geode, bottlenecked glass—
And then, inspiration!
A sudden wile! Borne on waves of adrenaline,
        I unscrewed the cap of the captive
Beefeater bottle and hoisted the turkey, as onto a palanquin,
All eighteen pounds, up on my shoulder. And sucked, an engine
On empty. Release. Freezing
Lethe. And its aftertaste, as just then
Carolyn had to shamble in.
        "You've got a problem,"
She said. I never invited that bitch again.

The only cure for excess is moderation, but hard drinkers reject preventative medicine. They seek salvation after the fact, the power of the placebo effect. Look it up and you'll find that *placebo* in Latin is the first-person singular future indicative of *placere*, to please, and translates to "I shall be pleasing or acceptable," exactly the words a hard drinker wants to hear the morning after. (*Placenta*, by the way, comes from the Latin for *cake*.) Those who face hangovers have developed a variety of faith-healing measures none of which shall be pleasing to the taste, a whiff of punishment being essential to their religion: drink a big glass of milk and Coca-Cola before bed, eat tripe or deep-fried canary for breakfast, drop a raw egg into a glass of tomato juice, or, by far the bitterest cure, knock back some Fernet-Branca. Only the hard core dare ingest it, or rabid believers in the medicinal value of revulsion.[6] Black and slightly thick, it begs, like motor oil, not to be consumed. Brits, who brought us Marmite, another substance of alarming appearance and consistency, swear that a shot of this foul substance first thing in the morning cures a hangover.

---

6. Given these properties, you'd think Fernet-Branca would be in the speed rack of every seedy rathole worth its neon sign, places like Paul's Lounge, where I'd go to meet a certain out-of-work drummer before wedded bliss asphyxiated my Lucky Strike-toting, wild-girl incarnation. At Paul's Lounge, the hard core and the rabid mingled freely with urban anthropologists like me under the penurious owner's gimlet eye. Nobody felt the need to keep up appearances, because nobody could see, the light was so dingy. And yet, I never heard a single call for Fernet-Branca, though there was plenty of moaning about hangovers. It's in the sort of upscale bistro where I tended bar that you find the kind of person who would order it: gallery owners, executive directors of foundations, Brazilians on their marathon holidays, Brits. Anyone who wears a Windsor knot over a secret history of TV dinners.

"Your pipes are caustic, ma'am." The plumber spoke
with courtesy reparative. Yet she knew
just what the handyman meant. Why, they've been through
so much, so much through them, no wonder they're broken,
she thought, or bitter. "Honey, after the highballs
they channeled last night, my pipes, no doubt unstinting
in their disregard, can't help their hinting
at character defects in their low-pitched squall."
They suffer, but suffering's so tedious
one can't make a living at it anymore.
Why don't they try stand-up, or Literary
Criticism—that smart-mouth esophagus,
bowels labyrinthine as a Borges library,
fallopian jokes. Hilarious, the gore.

As with raw emotion, serve Fernet-Branca in a shapely sherry glass far daintier than
what's in it.

The Barmen of Paul's Lounge Draft a Field Manual for Counterinsurgency

I. SHOW OF FORCE

Weapons are especially important. Unfortunately, there is widespread availability of weapons, with especially large surpluses in the most violent areas of the world.
   —Lieutenant General David H. Petraeus

Wild Turkey, Stolichnaya, Cuervo Gold
and other explosives siloed
on shelves behind us. Our plan:
water them down and hand
them out. We stack the rocks
glasses into cannonball pyramids. Clock strikes
mailman (he drinks Killian's) and Mission Creep stalks
in with his monthly VA check,
shakes a pen at the back, manages to ink
an EKG that once was his name.
Set him up, for shame,
a cache to drain the $129, minus
cashing fee for winos.
Down to the dimes, one last shot of rye
and shuffle him off to Broadway.
He'll catch the Night Train
Express, someone else's headache, bound for oblivion.
Creep used to joke on his way out, "Next comes the good stuff."
Now his speech, his laugh

don't translate to human.
Blistered mouth, pissed-on flag, shit stain, contusion.

II. PACIFICATION

Protracted popular war is the most successful insurgent strategy. The soldier must then be prepared to become a social worker, a civil engineer, a schoolteacher, a nurse, a boy scout. Human decency and the law of war require land forces to assist populations in their AOs.

The money starts rolling at 5:15.
Pool green, union green, bookie green, hooker green,
Joey Ramone drank here green. Once we arm the sectarian
rogues we knew they were, our tactics
shift toward Hippocratic, the way any acronym
might handle hearts and minds, ready with a diplomatic
soda back, a souvenir for children,
polite to death in our abbreviation.

Deploy patrols to notify the bullies
of bedtime. Tuck the unsteady
into taxicabs. Our duty mild and motherly
but always our barrels
feed the taps. The sweet spume of peril
could well up at any time, don't forget.
Fists could close, hand slide to pocket.
Bad luck to say *quagmire*
or let a woman behind the bar. In panic, shots are fired
or held. An innocent hits the sidewalk
to make his dark way down the block.

III. MOP-UP

Aware of the emotional toll that constant combat takes on their subordinates and the potential resulting psychoneurotic injury from cumulative stress or killing other human beings, caring leaders provide emotional "shock absorbers" for their subordinates. It is critical Soldiers and Marines have outlets to share their feelings and reach closure on traumatic experiences.

The bar amputates at the waist.
Few survive such illusions. How to end our standoff? Disgrace
is not an option on either side
of the spill zone, but it's no disgrace to give last call, and genocide
threatens the perimeter. Get out
by cutting off the juice. Get out by saying *Everybody get out.*
Then count the till. Turn the music lower.
Legs bunkered, bodies truncated: What's the best we could hope for,
hired guns? Look at us, how
they see us, star-spangled, though we could be in wheelchairs for all they know.

How to Make an Old Fashioned

Use the AO for mortar, a heavy-bottomed Old Fashioned glass, so that you won't have to transfer the remains. Improvise your pestle. Call up a sugar cube and dash of bitters, the human condition. Then a maraschino cherry. Then a few drops of water. Then a slice of orange. Mash them until the solids crash. The Old Fashioned winks nobly at its own vanishing appeal, as if a prisoner before a firing line, but it won't see any action until orange flesh merges with red, liquids and solids converge somewhere between liquid and solid, and entropy reigns over the mutual antagonism of the ingredients. "Surely that rough paste is how we look to God," cries the chaplain, who forgives us our infections as we forgive those who infest against us. The Old Fashioned is ready.[7]

(Interior Life of Tumbler:

Spare me the sweet sediment. Spare me the instant sour mix. Spare me
the flat beer of your sympathy. So I'm young, big deal, so I still weep in terror
at the insatiable whine of an Electrolux vacuum cleaner. I've got rent to pay,
extravagant emotions, a noisome hereafter grander and greedier
than you'll tap in our two days' acquaintance. Big deal,
my parents call Sundays, spare me, send mittens and clippings of high-
grade grubbers no thanks rubbing up to Security's leg like the one-eyed cat
I sat for two weeks of Ramen spare me Noodles. Nosebleed East Siders, spare
me the change from your Bencharong teacup, your Boshanlu censer, no sense my Bunsen
burner can't compete for hardwire heat I seek I seek I seek
truth and ye shall bruise.)

Pack ice on top of this mess, a medic with a terminal case, and dress it with whiskey, bourbon or rye. Work gently so as not to disturb the muddle. The customer decides when to stir, not you. Lay a thin blanket of club soda on the very top, a General Issue version of tucking in a grown man's body. Service is not a form of communication, since the server

---

7. I am nostalgic for a past I've never actually *had,* for seventeenth-century craft guilds, spelling bees in one-room schoolhouses, gloves over the elbow, for the wind in Genesis moving over the face of the waters, all before my time. If I leave my foxhole, there is no Beforehand to which I may return, only out-of-reach histories and childproof folkways.

gives attention without asking for any in return. Service is a subset of myth and therefore ominously unilateral, creative but prone to incursions of bellicose stealth and friendly fire.

Warning Label on Bottle of Boodles

This gin is flavored with JUNIPER berries, giving it a POISONOUS reputation. CONSULT your pediatrician. Call the HOTLINE. Juniper has ABUSIVE properties, many imagined, some real. RABBITS should avoid swallowing its needles, berries or stems. Also PREGNANT WOMEN, who should AVOID SWALLOWING needles, berries and stems altogether. INHALATION: Get fresh air immediately. Contact your representative. CLEAR and HOLD. You will be instructed. DO NOT use passive tense. Americans, this gin has been engineered to WARD away curious CHILDREN while cleansing the target area.[8]

---

8. During the first eight months of my pregnancy, I worked, hoisting cases of Amstel Light and garbage cans of ice right up until the point when I realized the sous-chef was interrupting his fricassee to help, busboys were staying late to stock the bar and waiters were steering their customers away from the few decent wines on our list, the ones kept in the tiny back cabinet made inaccessible by my ballooning midriff. I was costing them, so I took my leave. Homebound, I helped my husband clean out the crawl space behind the stairs where a previous tenant had left, amazingly, a car engine and some long pipes that might have been useful for offshore drilling, all of which we dragged piecemeal at 4 a.m. to an adjacent building where a dumpster, that urban rarity of large-scale disposal, had appeared, a miracle, like life itself.

Brewer's Yeast: A Lullaby

Plexus and hoodwinker, hoarding your leavening
springs in abominable cavities: yellow
your color is yellow, is twirlybird, wherewithal
swelter and swollen, conception inside me

as eggs dropped through chutes in a time kept obscurely:
your lunatic counterweight crippled and ceasing
to heal me, to whole me, to render me thus
had I kept to myself: you perplex me, my heliotrope,

pulling a shadow and pooling it noonward
one day in a bedroom, my amber limbs waning:
he brewed me, he bowed me, all boon and all boothale,
I brooded and knew what it was to draw breath,

my third chakra, my manpower, excess of energy:
now I grow big in devotion to mirrors,
reflecting on closets of clothes that don't fit
till I turn to the healing arts: cassia, peppermint,

lemongrass, thyme, and advice from a guru:
"For the bully, the judge, for the master of nothing
who harries your heartbeats, you treat him with violets
followed by one brief lacuna of yellow."

Spirits

Here is some advice from the *Oxford American Dictionary* (edited by Eugene Ehrlich et al., Oxford University Press, New York, 1980): "Do not confuse *spiritual* with *spirituous*." The latter means loaded with alcohol, the former with soulfulness, which the latter, some say, instills, though the dictionary seems keen to separate the two conditions, maintaining a distinction between distilling spirits and instilling spirit.[9] No semantic knot can be severed succinctly, just as no drink can be unmixed.

9. On my birthday, I came home to an empty apartment. No surprise, until I opened the door to our bedroom. It was filled with balloons. Balloons in extravagance, hundreds of them, a balloon cocktail (rye, Pernod, sweet vermouth, orange bitters, egg white) which danced and reeled around the place for weeks, half Plath's "Oval soul-animals," half an untraceable recipe. How our child will love these, I thought, even as they puckered and dried. Then my water broke. After considerable conflict, we named her Marguerite.

Malted Barley

You often confuse Ceres, the goddess of grain,
with that ardent seeker, Demeter. My bed may be cold, but my cradle
is full, my breakfast already eaten from a porcelain bowl white
as a cranium, clean as a break or a vow at the top stair cracked
before your shoes can sound their steel-tipped descent from flights
where you now nightly sleep.

How do you sleep? I wonder how you sleep.
Each morning our evening's rage ingrains
itself in my telling of it to myself: the pearl a crusty oyster shell cradles
so defensively, the shallow grave of white
lies I give my estranged and crack-
pot heart, a breakfast ceremony as boring as an osprey's circular flight

when there's nothing to eat. You reheat leftovers too, of fight-or-flight
instinct, and this, our entrapment, the childproof bars on the cradle
upstairs belied by the child inside who only seems to sleep
through our boiling spats. At two, she's cracked
the code of discord. You don't believe me, but she's tasted of Hades a grain
or two, she has. I've seen her bite, just as I've seen your white

knuckles go against the grain
of that calm you claim won't crack
but always does. Our child, Persephone of sleep,
abstains from waking. I take that time to read, a book cradled

in my arms and heavier than her heavy head, with its off-white
hair so feather fine, so prone like mine to flight.

Ceres never had Demeter's devotion. I cradle
my empty bowl in my treacherous palms, some whole-wheat grain
still stuck to its white
lip where a chip is the delta to a hairline crack
too thin for tributaries. To take flight
upriver, to rid by bleaching, to sleep, to sleep.

But I will fill the bowl again, and bring forth grain
the way a goddess will, and leave the harvest to sleep
late, cradle
to outgrow itself. I'm fixed in flight
from all but conception, cerebral words like seeds in a white
envelope. How maternal, this spoon, its practical click clink crack

and the clean white milk that sleeps
in it. How cracked, the jettison, the grain
scooped up in slow flight from a porcelain-skulled cradle.[10]

---

10. When Marguerite (Pearl! Crumb! Little Daisy! Oxeye!) was but hours old, I received instruction
from a severe RN at the hospital to nurse her every three hours "lest ye die" and, along with
that stricture, a few useless tips for waking up a baby who didn't want to wake up: tickle her
feet, chuck her under the chin, blow on her face, taking care to support her head. Most new
moms pray for respite; for the next two weeks I was doing the opposite, setting my alarm for
midnight, then 3 a.m., then six, lurching out of bed like a crazed prophet, rousting my infant with

continued

Progress Report from Tiny Neglected Dears Day Care Center

For lunch your child had: pease porridge hot, your mother's coming soon _____ .

For snack your child had: pease porridge cold, your mother's gone again _____ .

Today your child: ____ drew a circle

                        ____ hopped on one foot

                        ____ said *motherfucker*

                        ____ made Sophie cry by pretending to be a space alligator
who screams *your mother is never coming*

At Craft Time we: made an ashtray out of body parts _____ .

At Circle Time we: read *The Runaway Bunny*, all lies, all lies, your mother
is never coming _____ .

Reminder: Pickup time is when we say it is sharp! _____ .

Signed,

     You're not a real mother. My real mother is a rabbit _____ .

---

textbook tickles, chucks and puffs to coax her into latching on. These devotions went on with almost no nursing on her part—she stayed serenely insensible—but with plenty of weeping and gnashing of teeth on mine, amplified through sleep deprivation, until an astonished pediatrician ("You're doing *what*? Waking her up?") mercifully said, "My God, let her sleep!"

Blue Moon

Nightly you freeze my child from sleep, afraid
Of moonshot light
Rightly feared, I say. That is no way

To behave,
You marble stare, you cold bedspread,
You crystal wave.

You ought to be ashamed, but, see,
You settle instead,
The mother you are not, not even a she,

And possibly
Even you regret the misattribution,
That lunar tune.

Midas in reverse, you turn tabletop
And run, silver
Madness all over the room, amok,

Chilled, too eerie
To be drunk. From her crib she fingers
Your bad aim

Until I enter, her more real mother,
Mouthing theories
To return each foreign object to its name:

This is your lamp,
Your quilt. This is paper, just paper—
Words fly the slant

White rhyme her face makes with mine.
I elide to shadow,
an unlettered ghost, but you, I remind

You, have yet
To loosen your influence, tinnitus singing
nightly, *Ill met, ill met.*

SWING SHIFT

When I started this job, I gloried in specialized stemware, the functionality of a snifter, the shape that a martini comes in, so angular and pushy, so flared. I gloried in lore, too. There's no point in ignoring the fabled past. Once upon a time, martini proportions were different, with fully a third of the drink vermouth. It surprises people now, who have come to consider vermouth a liability. I used to make martinis the old-fashioned way over customers' objections, in stubborn attachment to what I thought of as a barkeep's integrity, a vow to love, to cherish, to honor tradition. Back then it hurt to yield to a patron's declared taste, to deny them what was mine to give, good design. Back then I had an impossibly misjudged long view. Now, I've broken my vows so often, I barely consider the burn a dry martini leaves. I reach for the cheap stuff, service with a shrug.

Still, here I am in my stainless white shirt. I could rouse myself to pour a jigger of white wine and two jiggers of gin over cracked ice to chill. I could decline to shake it, though not because it bruises the liquor, a myth even I have managed to shed. I could pack a martini glass with ice and a little water and go do something thoughtful while it got cold. Maybe I would give someone I once knew a quick head rub.[11] Then I would let three small-to-medium sized olives drift down into the glass, down to the bottom, like a marriage falling down the stairs slowly.

---

11. He loved my fingers on his temples, on his thinning hair, on the base of his skull. He loved the stealth, spontaneity, territorial roam, my nails lightly scratching but ready to fend. The last time my fingers touched him, he said, "Can you not do that," and I went to bed, though I could have poured myself out so precisely that, even with the melt from the ice in which I'd chilled, the contents of the shaker would have filled him exactly to the rim, maybe even a little over the rim, so that only the surface tension of the liquid kept it from spilling over.

Pink Lady

She ordered her gin as if it were a hat,
sawdust were wall-to-wall fresh-vacuumed plush
and Red behind the bar, a milliner.

He'd shake the cocktail, beefy forearms raised,
two fat pincushions bleeding flesh-tone freckles,
and pour the pink foam up to the elegant rim

where the broken imprint of yesterday's lipstick
hung tough, not quite washed out, whispering
of former shades: Palace Pink, Passionberry Stain,

Torrid Rose. Things fade. Vivid things fade
the most. Upstairs the washed-up neon sign
kept spelling, spelling, spelling SRO.

A Prayer on Wide-Ruled Paper[12]

The topic is narrow and manageable
Her living room sheds white fringe, unraveling one swatch at a time.

Reasonably accurate details are present to support the main ideas
Even the blue love seat, damask, distresses itself thread by thread.

The writing attempts to connect with the audience in an earnest, pleasing, but impersonal manner
She sees shabbiness gaining. Mom? Dad? She puts her head on her arms.
Destiny would be just fine, if it weren't so predictable.

Transitions sometimes work; at other times, connections between ideas are unclear
Today, the mourning doves sound canned. Cassettes, their coos pop and hiss.
The LPs Dad no longer plays collect warp in basement stacks.
Too, the stairs pop and hiss with dust, for they're always headed down.

Prayers of the People

I once asked Red where all his friends were. "Half of them quit drinking," he said cheerfully, "the other half are dead." Church attendance at the Temple is slipping, yet

---

12. Language is the refuge of the optimist. Only the future child of divorce (O Marguerite! The Lord taketh pleasure in his people; he will beautify the meek with salvation!) knows otherwise. The rest of us have faith that we author our sordid destinies. He might have left me, a regular switching loyalties with ruthless ease, but I cling to my solace: it was I who fraternized with the customer. It was I who bore her. I gave her this taint we call life and she could not have it any other way.

Red has never denied the Bread and Wine to a parishioner, not even a dead one. All are welcome at his Holy Table. The drinkers in his lexicon are like vowels in the Alphabet. He doesn't make sense without them. Something about Red—maybe his read on people, judgment without Contempt—makes him the preferred host to that vanishing breed, the Daytime Drinker. We get a regular set of them here, none beautiful, none particularly Lucrative or even interesting, but nonetheless, none a bad way to ease through lunch. "Painkillers come and go but pain stays in style," he reasons. Then come the Intercessions, for authority, welfare, those in Any Trouble, and the departed:

Red's Prayer for the Old Fashioned

Muddling is a lost art, or losing one,
I should say. Pestle, mortar, proportions
of fruit to bitters, sugar to spritz.
These young ones are hired for their looks
while what gets lost, I ask you?

It's like that bread they don't know
how to make anymore, just its name
and the fact that it existed. Old
Fashioned, sure. Look at that guy:
carnation boutonniere, fedora.

Comes in every Friday looking sharp,
alone, and who knows what he knows?
He might have been the president
of some company, or a scientist, or kid
at Wrigley Field when Babe called

his shot, which is where I grew up,
Chicago, and the only A I ever got
in school was 7th grade, Life Science,
Mrs. Hoffman said it was my gift.

Have compassion on those who suffer from any Grief or trouble.
That they may be Delivered from their distress.

Red's Prayer for the Rusty Nail

An old man's drink
in an old man's hand
stiff with scotch and

Drambuie, amber glower
culled from what's left
after gut-rot scotch

and sweetened to tolerable.
Hangover appeased,
his hand should relax

its clench on the glass
but doesn't. *See how
crooked my fingers got,*

*like they never stopped
working?* And corroded,
maybe tossed in the grass,

left there too long, as if
once driven in bent, 'taint
worth hammering straight.

Give to the departed Eternal rest.

Red's Prayer for Mister Mudslide

A portly gent, dressed in his oxford shirts,
fat, sure, but he deserved a handle with
some honorific splash, and so we dubbed
him "Mister Mudslide," add a touch of class
to an otherwise shabby spot, our freaky cook

obsessed with sprouts and wheat germ, equal parts
health food and rats, graffiti and smoothie shakes.
He'd come weekdays, usually afternoons,
mild-mannered fellow, quiet, no trouble t'all—
the junkies are polite, I'll give 'em that.

Soon as he lumbered in, I'd know his order:
Mudslide. Always the same. And though he showed
up every day, he'd tiptoe to the bar
all strangerly. *Excuse me, sir* (he must
have known my name was Red) *Excuse me, sir,*

I'll have a mudslide, please.
And then he'd nod

his head and I'd nod mine, to signify
we understood each other, see. He'd tuck
some bills under his cocktail napkin, and off
he'd roll to shoot up in the men's room stall.

Now, mudslides are like milkshakes, messy and sweet.
They taste like you're not drinking alcohol,
which tells you why they're popular with the kids
or ladies who would rather have dessert
but can't because they're watching what they eat,

though mudslides might as well be crème brûlée.
For me, I never cared for them. Too sweet.
Plus once a person orders one of those,
the whole bar has to have 'em, like a—well,
a mudslide.
                    This is how your trends get started.

Before you know it, you've got dirty glasses
stacked to here, and you can't get them clean
because of all that cream clouding your washwater.
Mister Mudslide, though, I didn't mind.
He mostly showed up in the afternoon

when no one's starting trends, at least in bars.
So like I said, I'd make the drink while he'd go
do his business, fifteen, twenty minutes,

however long it took to get his high,
then back to his stool already looking droopy.

And now the waitresses would all come 'round
the service end to see the Mudslide Show.
This guy, poor slob, would brace himself against
the bar and slowly elevate his glass,
but just before he got it to his lips—

I mean the instant just before the sip—
he'd nod out, battening his eyelid hatches,
mudslide listing like a battleship,
about to spill, the glass midair, him fighting
hard, a drowning man, bobbing and jerking.

But here's the miracle of Mister Mudslide:
he could hold that drink in his limp fingers,
he'd hold it on the very verge of sheer
catastrophe, for minutes at a time
while smack suspended him somewhere between

defiance of and compliance with the laws
of gravity.
                    Just when we thought he'd lost
control at last, he'd come to with a snort
and set the glass back down, the sip still

unconsummated.

Then he'd start again.

Riveting. We couldn't help but watch.
This was his life, and ours, a waiting game.
A bigger waste of art you've never seen.
He didn't spill his mudslide that I saw,
but then he never drank it neither.

How to Make a Mudslide

After you've worked here about a year, you'll realize you've been sliding slowly downhill the whole time. The floor is uneven, you see? It took me that long to notice.[13] I could make this nightcap in my sleep, the recipe is so symmetrical: equal measures of vodka, coffee liqueur and Irish cream, two sweets and a tart, all poured over ice and shaken, listlessly. The only trick is to strain the mudslide into a glass that's bigger than you'd expect. Any cream-based ingredient, anything cloudy, expands with shaking. The volume goes up at the end of the night, even though you're so tired you wouldn't think you'd bother fighting.

---

13. We'd made it through dinner with "friends," and although there was some mutual sniping I doubt it registered with them, busy as they were with their tales of market research. We had no exit strategy, my newish husband and I, and so advanced together to the "little spot" our "friends" knew where we could continue our "talk" comfortably. And he called for one of those horrific eaux de vie, grappa, some such thing. And I ordered a mudslide, in honor of our sluggish destruction.

Tickled Pink

Pink secretes satin heart-shaped pillows of no known
utility, lace trim on valentines, excess tulle

on little girls queening it over little girls at pageants.
There would be no babies without its squealing

delusion of joy, no teens in dark parked cars, older boys
drinking Tickled Pink from its faux-champagne bottle,

pulling your striped tights down to your high-heeled
sandals with golden starfish embedded in the vinyl straps.

What other girls are doing gets you through the first time
in cold blood: his flat stomach and father's waterbed

slap at you from both sides, quiet despite the thrush-quick
twinges; how clammy, abrasive, tight-lipped this labor.

The lubricant is mostly empty now, lying on its side,
its green-glass nozzle aimed at phallicism.

At the corner of your mouth a festive froth gathers, pink,
newly tinged, like the bubbles will be in your late-night bath.

How to Make a Pink Lady

There's a certain class of drinks—the "nicer" class, ordered by the "nicer" lady drinkers—that are made with the whites of eggs. Naturally, they are labor-intensive, but as we know, labor is the currency of respect. The names alone of these concoctions bespeak a lifestyle thick with first-class travel and memberships in garden clubs: Waterbury. Calm Voyage. Bird of Paradise. Diamond Head. Chanticleer. Via Veneto. There are even some perfectly fine colleges to be considered: Cornell Cocktail, Lafayette, Carolina, in a pinch. And behold the manicured beatitude of a September Morn, Morning Glory Fizz and Pink Rose, which is the same thing as a Pink Lady, gin, cream, lemon, but with slightly less grenadine.

Interruption by Singapore Sling

My daughter is falling, is falling from catalpas,
from monkey bars, piano benches, is falling
in barbeque pits at playdates, St. Patrick's Day parties,
she's falling out of bed, she's sleeping and flung.

What startles, that paisley rugs and asphalt alike
could volunteer her embrace? In flight from infant
dread, a Moro reflex plays her six years
obsessively. Her arms parachute open,

but where down should be is gravity's unbroken
surface, and off to Dr. Grace go humerus,

clavicle, carpals. The parts add up to spirit
lemon-laced and cordial: a sling for heartbreak

palpated, not to be healed of shrapnel and flack
no jacket dissuades. My daughter is falling back
into her Good Girl routine, a junior drill team
officer doing her backover port spin best

with a sequined rifle. Outside weather's clear,
but trauma embeds itself like fractured bone,
cracked ice, lightning deep in a Homer seascape.
She's falling into reverie, slinging Together

with cherry Get Back into a gulf you'd call hope
if it hadn't been drained long ago, and not by her.
She's just a falling daughter, floating brandy
shot at high velocity, stone in a Singapore sling.

Start with that egg. I love eggs. I love their density, their unblemished shape. I love
separating the white from the yolk, using the shell itself as a kind of natural strainer.
Bobbling that resilient blob of yellow back and forth from one half to another, I believe
anew in Ionic order, or, if not order, exactly, then an ancient justice handed down, a
noblesse oblige. Once I've segregated the egg, I squeeze half of a lemon. Now, I pour the
juice over cracked ice into a shaker, add a splash of cream, the egg white and the gin, and
enough grenadine to blush it pink. Then I shake it, not so much in anger, though there is
anger, or resentment at the way things turned out—I do not yet know how things will

turn out—as in the sense of lost possibility, or preventing lost possibility, in a kind of fervor of thoroughness, lest there be any unshaken bits left. I shake to make things smooth, for I, too, am a lady.[14]

---

14. Sometimes I creep upstairs to check on my daughter and her hair is plastered to her head with sweat and it's so *fine*, it looks like a membrane, she looks like a dead animal, or an unborn one, but then I remember how I looked before I took this job, dressed up in campy headscarves, green satin heels, all alligator and sequins and lavender gloves to the elbow. One night it was an Audrey Hepburn number with a little jacket, my hair teased; his eyebrows like caret marks, like cartoon eyebrows expressing cartoon surprise, our noticing of each other, our signals flashy as gold lamé, and I think, *That's* what's real, the cartoon outside is real, this hot sleeping thing is not. So I shake her. This violence is not violation, I reason. I must upset it to teach it equilibrium. Who could bear a glister of egg white, slapped like saliva against the glass? Who could bear such a display? Her face crumpled, her rage like a slept-in bed, no: a Pink Lady must have peace.

Shirley Temple

In this poem, Mae West sweeps onto the stage.
She hunts down Shirley Temple's starstruck mother,
draws blood, a union card, and burns the frosting

contract to shoot ten films this year.
It's 1934. Mae shouts, "Confect
no more, my midget queen of vamp, who dips

apneatically through lyrics, peppering hics
like instant mousse, too frozen cute a flirt
to pucker those bee-starved lips." Mae puts up cash

for moms who never ask, "Why aren't you sweet
like Shirley?" Shirley taps the migrant's feet,
plays the sods of bust. The stompers stammer

but never hit the beat. They trip along
with Shirley, faith in flash, good ships of state
and stay the course on 25 cents an hour.

They learn her résumé, the hobbies, husbands.
The migrant daughters patch their Mae West boots
to pay for Shirley atop a wedding cake.

Imagine wealth. Imagine impulse buys. Imagine saying, Let's get both.[15] Now try facing the opposite challenge: imagine hunger, imagine orphanages, imagine having to end the Depression all by your curly-top self without a good stiff drink. Shirley Temple the child star faked hardship for a living, just as Shirley Temple the mix of ginger ale and grenadine fakes alcohol content. Therefore, to make a Shirley Temple, you must pray the *Magnificat*, the Song of Mary, a series of contradictions designed either to transcend paradox or to break the supplicant's will on it. "My soul doth magnify the Lord," but also "For he that is mighty hath magnified me." There's a braggadocio in "For behold, from henceforth : all generations shall call me blessed" that's hard to reconcile with "the lowliness of his handmaiden" in the line before. Perhaps it is not intentional, but the *Magnificat* also contains a plot synopsis for every film in Shirley Temple's oeuvre:

> He hath put down the mighty from their seat : and hath exalted the humble and
>   meek.
> He hath filled the hungry with good things : and the rich he hath sent empty
>   away.

---

15. On Cheap Days ("Lent meets Rent") we feast on Kraft Macaroni & Cheese, the Cheesiest, with or without frozen peas mixed in. We hit the library, where at 4:15 kids ages 4–6 can create their own seascapes by gluing shells, sand, tiny starfish and blue glitter to tagboard. But we really get our money's worth playing the wig game: I pretend the dishtowel on my head is a fancy hairdo in the Louis XIV style, and I say "La di da di da, look at my exquisite wig" in a hoity-toity voice until my daughter snatches it away and tears off into the den, upon which I chase her, shrieking, "My wig! My wig! Give me my wig!" and trap her between the sofa and bookshelf and tickle her to get it back.

She made millions playing this story. Which leaves bartenders with a moral quandary: Do we serve or do we *pretend* to serve? Do we make drinks, keeping the law, or make them up? Then we are the proud he hath scattered in the imagination of their hearts, and so we garnish a Shirley Temple with a maraschino cherry and plant a free straw in it, the bendy kind which can double as a periscope for the submarine ride home.

Bull's Blood

We must have idled at eight different package stores
That night, our not-quite-legal eyebrows darkly raised

At your father's quest for sacrifice, frenzy, murder:
Wine so seductive, chalices widen their mouths,

Dreaming alone in their curtained sacristies,
He slavered of it, a wine that had Hungarians

Beating the ground, oak calluses like casks,
St. Donat's Day. We settled into a backseat night

To watch him, engorged, returning empty-fisted
From each neon paradise, then felt the slam

Of drive and park, until he charged the next,
Only to emerge as if he'd been stabbed.

Under his nose we purpled, our blood grew ripe.
Our scents grew sharp on tar, gas fumes and sweat,

Our swollen taste-buds glistened in our spit.
We too were thirsty, driven to drink red depths.

Bloody Mary

The Bloody Mary is the meatloaf of cocktails. It cannot be overseasoned, in my opinion, and a kind of everything-but-the-kitchen-sink spirit prevails over it like warm wind over the tropics. Where else do horseradish and celery salt, tomato juice and lime, Worcestershire and Tabasco harbor in such amiable partnership? A good Bloody Mary negotiates the consistency of vichyssoise and its bounty to boot, except in matters spirituous. Having bought round after round for last night's after-hours tipfest, I am obligated out of house-conscious karma to short today's drinkers their vodka. A well-made Bloody Mary will never tell how much (or little) vodka she contains. You can count on her.[16]

---

16. Where did the money go? I worked. He worked. Our rent-controlled apartment was embarrassingly cheap, not much more than Thoreau's cabin as totted up in *Walden* (p. 46):

Boards	$8 03½	Mostly shanty boards.
Refuse shingles for roof and sides	4 00	
Laths	1 25	
Two second-hand windows with glass	2 43	
One thousand old brick	4 00	
Two casks of lime	2 40	That was high. More than I needed.
Hair	0 31	
Mantle-tree iron	0 15	
Nails	3 90	
Hinges and screws	0 14	
Latch	0 10	
Chalk	0 01	
Transportation	1 40	I carried a good part on my back.
In all	$ 28 12½	

continued

Beyond housing, our other living expenses went something like this:

Groceries	$57 79	Why do you always buy the generic brand? Get the good stuff.
Insurance	76 61	
Cleaning	34 61	Forget doing it yourself. We need a professional.
Home Improvement	129 16	
Telephone	35 47	
Baby Equipment	32 62	That was high.
Charity	10 28	What a waste.
Books	8 22½	More than you needed.
Miscellaneous	202 74	

Miscellaneous. That was our single biggest expense. Miscellaneous. Miscellaneous was working late and called away for the weekend. Miscellaneous was drop off his blue oxfords at the laundry because I incorrectly creased the cuffs when I tried to iron them. Miscellaneous was club dues. Miscellaneous was his spontaneous purchase one Saturday of Eames bookshelves, a domain name and a mantle-tree iron. Miscellaneous was a dozen lilies for Mother's Day, each as heavy as a scepter, exhaling a scent powerful enough to brainwash the bearer or restore her to the throne after a bloody civil war. Marguerite had been feverish, her intermittent cries like a meat grinder, for nearly a week. Since Tuesday I'd had 9 hours of sleep and ¾ of a strawberry banana yogurt. I was weepy. I needed help. "Couldn't you take a day off instead of sending flowers?" I'd sobbed.

"Don't you get it?" he'd shouted. "I have to work. I *have* to work. *Someone* has to put the roof over your head. We can't pay the electric bill in *poems*, for chrissake."

Before long, we were glowering like a couple of red-hot mantle-tree irons and our formerly loveable quirks (she's soooo creative; he's soooo passionate) came pounding down like one thousand old bricks on our newly sanded hardwood floors ($2,886.15). "You book-vomiting maw of chaos!" "You flyting joisthead!" Slam. Silence. Somewhere else, down at the Red Crosse, maybe at Mead Hall, Miscellaneous was buying.

Steaming Bull

I am not some piece of graffiti. I am
not some eighteenth-century huckleberry.
When I cut do I not bleed more than
it hurts her? I am not some grog, some stir fry,
not some tattling Ked. An outrage, how
she cripples my Dry Clean Only socks. Water
rings on vanities! And felt-tip pens
on vanities! I'm not some varsity bellhop.
Her blah blah friends, she lets them talk her into
outrageous drapes she hangs without permission!
She always. Never. Asks. And *gosh*. Stop saying
gosh I say, stop baking pumpkin bread,
stop touching the walls so late at night, stop flossing
in echo-y rooms. But here's the kicker, here's the
smash, see, here's the doppelgänging bust:
she won't communicate. Stop tap-tap-tapping at
legal pads. I'm not some poetry husband.

This cheap date of a cocktail wears too much makeup. Even the name is fake. What masquerades as sexual innuendo turns out to be the recipe for the drink: "Slow" is for sloe gin, "Comfortable" is for Southern Comfort—tell me if I'm speaking too shrewdly, too lewd-ish—and "Screw" is for screwdriver, that most common of beverages.

First I put the screwdriver to bed: a little vodka, a little more orange juice in a Collins glass packed with ice. Then I slap a little sloe gin in there, making it blush, as if it had shame. Lastly I top off the glass with Southern Comfort. Let that crude heckle of a customer stir it herself. Am I speaking too loudly, too baft, too stuttersome? If I were following a recipe instead of my instinct, I'd shake the three liquors before I mixed in the orange juice. As if there were something here to improve. Ha. Ha, ha, ha. This drink isn't worthy of getting my professional wares dirty.

Still Life of Slow Comfortable Screw

Like a felon she spreads her legs
at the mirror in the Ladies' Lounge.

Her wristwatch clinks manacle-style
as she flicks her hair from a hooped ear.

---

17. The grounds for divorce in New York State are delightfully archaic: *abandonment*, for the helpless; *cruelty*, a wonderfully ambiguous term that describes all marriages—even happy ones—at some curve in the matrimonial track; and *adultery*. No ambiguity there. Either he did or he didn't. Or did he?

Her roots are coming in: Ronkonkoma,
no matter how she backcombs and sprays

the row house looms, hot upper rooms,
hot breath of a stepbrother, a cousin,

then the row of boys from grammar school,
each with his anxiety, a soft small gerbil

to be petted, each with his tremors.
Juvenile stuff, not like now in her full power,

the club lights hammering, sirens, scramble,
the grown men hasty, she smashed on blackthorn.

Not so fast. As with cheating husbands, certain cocktails have developed strategies to deceive themselves and others into thinking that they are innocent of alcohol, have never commingled their juices with vodkas, wouldn't dream of letting a bottle get between their rosy legs. Liars and dissolutes, all, easily busted by their callow names: a variant of the above is the Slow Comfortable Screw Against the Wall (just add Galliano, of Harvey Wallbanger fame, and you can do it standing up, maybe in a toilet stall, someplace comfortable like that). Then there's Sex on the Beach, Glad Eyes, Daddy, Don't Make Me Drink This, Hot Pants, Woo-Woo. The Queen Slut of such mendacity is the Long Island Iced Tea, emphasis on Long Island. It has practically every type of booze in the speed rack but still comes out tasting like an instant-powder version of that classic summertime cooler. The only intoxicants a Long Island Iced Tea leaves out are whiskey and scotch, the telltale lipstick stains on a collar. Even amateurs avoid those. Especially amateurs, that is, since the typical drinker of these debauched punches is either underage or otherwise interested in deniability, while serious drinkers embrace their sad art.

Also as with cheating husbands, everyone who comes near a Slow Comfortable Screw loses: the dishonored drinker, the ridiculous-tasting drink and the deceived one—in this analogy, me, the bartender who made it and thought that once I'd done my appalling job, I was absolved. *Au contraire*. Drink deep the bitterness of irony! The Slow Comfortable Screw will rematerialize on the service bar, an anxiety dream, with the following complaint duly conveyed by the waiter:

"There's no alcohol in this thing."

I will explain that the drink is *designed* to taste as if it had no alcohol in it. That's the point, so that the Slow, Comfortable Screwee won't taste the alcohol. The waiter will give me that forbearing you'll-see waiter look he gives everybody and whisk the despicable confect away. Minutes later he'll return with the same litany. The Screwing going on here is not Comfortable, although it's certainly Slow. I will cling to reason, as if Ronkonkoma were a stoa in ancient Greece and not a strip mall of Dollar Store libidos. I'll offer to come out from behind the bar and talk to the customer myself. The waiter will gleefully call my bluff. Out I'll go, brimming with expertise, ready to erase the specials on the chalkboard so I can diagram the chemical reaction whereby sloe gin, Southern Comfort and vodka react with orange juice to fake the nonalcoholic orgasm that is a Slow Comfortable Screw. Here's what she'll say:

"At T.G.I. Friday's I can taste the alcohol."

Admit defeat. I concede that, yes, I ought to put some liquor in that thing. But the war slogs on. She's an amateur. She probably thinks the swizzle stick is a straw. I carry the drink back to the bar and drizzle a single drop of vodka down the hollow of the swizzle stick. Bam! I've got her. On her first sip she'll taste nothing but alcohol. Though it be less than an eyedropper's worth, yet it is enough: her needs are psychological, not factual. Satisfaction will spread over her, will drape her like the 14-carat gold heart pendant the last married man shoved into her hands before crawling back to his degraded wife.

See what I mean? A Slow Comfortable Screw is everybody's loss. Some bartenders—maybe the ones at T.G.I. Friday's—tamper with the swizzle stick when they make the drink, before it's served, before the recipient has had a chance to taste it, much less complain that it's "not strong enough." These warriors of the Long Island set have learned what they need to survive: frivolous cocktails will always be your enemy, but some wars are not worth fighting. Placation. I should have known to dope and lube at the first complaint.

Sea Breeze

So I said to Rocco—he's been really good,
        considering the turbans
Bucky makes of everything: rash guards,
his Cub Scout neckerchief, and let's not forget

Marigold's wedding! Bless him, Rocco took
a deep, deep breath and croaked out, "Bucky, you look
        beautiful in that dress."
I said to Rocco, "The boy's not right down there,

I saw it in a documentary."
So I rented *La Cage aux Folles*, and he felt better,
          we all felt better,
and I thought, We can lick this thing. For once,

Rocco said, "Beats me. You can decide."
They have this operation, you know. The boy's
          wanted to be a girl
since forever, before he could talk, and now he's five

he practically comes out and says sex change,
I swear. "Bucky, set the table." "Sex change."
          So in this other
documentary, they had this transgendered—

that's what they call it—transgendered prostitute
who got it done, and he—or she?—was saying
          "Now I'm gaining weight."
So there's the downside, except the prostitute

was forty-two and Bucky's only five.
Still, maybe we should wait. But then again,
          you know Marigold's daughter?
No, the other one with the drummer boyfriend?

Well, she just landed a national commercial
to relaunch Cocoa Freakies, some cereal,
          and they pay girls more,
they really do. It's totally unfair.

On Giving Correct Change

As the day wears on and the somewhat tame lunch crowd devolves into the so-called happy hour, danger unsheathes its antennae, for the sharks have begun to circle and they attack without shame. My personal favorites were a pair of fake nuns who arrived in a whirl of gypsy black and fluttering, dog-eared, illegible identification badges, galloped through the bar and demanded donations with such aggression people would give before they had time to notice either the vague nature of the solicitation or the fraudulence of the cause-bearers. Part of my job—really, most of my job—is to protect the drinker from the consequences of his own acts. And so I hustled the hustlers out quickly and without remorse, over invocations of direst doom and protests of Old Testament dimensions. You may find as I did after ejecting these particular hucksters that you lose a paying customer or two, the Sea Breeze–drinking secretary who gapes and stutters, "You just threw out a *nun*," and never fully recovers from the shock to enjoy her libation. So be it. Unfortunately, while the Sea Breeze drinker never returned, one of the fake nuns did. Clearly her circumstances had been reduced even further than whatever destitution or drug habit had brought her to impersonating clergy. She was wearing a wimple crafted out of a garbage bag.

It's funny, it's sad, but never underestimate the ingenuity of desperation. There are the prestidigitators, who flash twenty-dollar bills for which you make change, never to realize you've been given a single. There are the dine-and-dashers, found in several species. First are primitive organisms called college kids who literally run out the door. These you chase or recruit waiters to chase; they are drunk and easily caught and have the money to pay and only neglected to produce it on a dare or other such peer-driven temporary insanity. The more advanced specimens, working alone, are the ones who "suddenly remember" they've left their keys in the car door or baby in the car seat, or who have been banking your sympathy ("When my second foster mother died . . .") in the hope you won't withdraw it when that moment of truth, the tab, arrives. The latter are expert, often sidesplitting tale-spinners. That, plus moral bankruptcy, ought to have paved their way to a successful career in politics, but they are alcoholic or damaged or just plain lazy, and so no such success has materialized.

Some of these desperadoes you will want to save. You see the humanity! the humanity! The person's verifiably intelligent or charming or has promise. Don't even try. You can't save anyone from the troubles they brew outside your purveyance, although this recognition that you're powerless and essentially uninformed will have to map itself in your brain through your own brushes with the chronically unreliable, those explorers who come back with wildly inaccurate maps, if they come back at all. I got my education from a charismatic I'll call Katy Z.

Here Are Lions

The map above the bar says Venture Not. Maps prefer dry
land to your unfinished screenplay about a biker chick who drinks
herself to death, which you plug to the producer one stool over.

Here are Dragons. The sunk costs of your sea legs affect
your stroll. The dragon has bitten, for what it's worth these days.
Here are Accountants and Men in Squamaceous Suits. You bear scars

nobody else appraises. You're broke, *but in a groovy-hippie way,*
you think, cracked black leather jacket like a child
beggar tugging at your shoulders and hips, those infernal

cowboy boots veering into the Scop and Bard for a shot of Jack—
Here are Pedophiliac Uncles—which you knock back sharply
while reaching for an anecdote about the Geats from your Military

History seminar in lieu of sous for Bill the barman. A tip of arrows
and on to the next convivium, a bit darker than the last, thicker
with uncertain mainstays, Wen-Necked Tars, shark-like creatures. Waves

over your head now. Here are Veterans of Bad Wars. Here are
Pedicular Junk Store Owners. *We're overdue for a Mae West revival*,
you shout, and hum a few bars, sparring with the Marxist (Groucho)

one stool over. (*I'm remarkable, he thinks*, you think, captain
of this sinking enterprise.) Here are Kept To Themselves. No one bothers
to shut the door behind him, the come and go is superficial that way

at the Shining Needle. You say very little, concentrate
on steering which is difficult because of the booms and jibs, they
seem to swing, the roars sundering. Here are Lions, bright lions.

NIGHT SHIFT

When you make a Negroni, stir it in a glass cocktail shaker instead of a metal one. You'll enjoy the view, watching the colors swirl together like a sunset, cynically.[18]

---

18. "You can't wait to get rid of me," he would snarl, but in the end, it was he who dissolved the marriage.

We'd long been reduced to one-celled television-watching globules in the absence of other animations. Of late, even our daughter had failed to roust us, although she'd certainly tried. It was about 8 p.m., Marguerite had finished her bath, had finished dancing naked with the light sneakers, her words for dust motes, and was busy sleeping in Tiny Mogul Pose, which involved lacing her little fingers behind her encephalitic head in unintentional imitation of Donald Trump. We sat afore the TV in Defeated Slug Pose, staring at the meaningless early minutes of an NBA game between two modestly talented but poorly coached teams. The buzzer rang. I jumped to assume Service Mentality Pose, rushing to the door, while he maintained Defeated Slug. Or had he shifted slightly into Flyswatter?

At the door stood a strange man in an orange trench coat the color of Marguerite's spit-up the first time she had truly vomited in the adult sense. She'd awakened, astonished and appalled at the news of it, squinched herself into a corner of the crib and pointed at it as if it were some shameful, punishable failure on her part. How to explain vomit to a two-year-old? How to explain it to grown-ups, for that matter, that such acrid debuts lie within, waiting for their involuntary ejaculation? The trench coat at the door identified itself in some officious way I don't recall but which I'm sure involved the word "ma'am." It asked me my name declamatorily, as if the question were so rhetorical it had become a statement: "Are you Your Name."

"Yes," I declaimed back.

The stranger handed me an envelope and turned away, one blobby hand reaching for the handrail that flattened itself like a fugitive alongside the rickety steps down. I backed into the apartment, looking to Flyswatter there in his pose, knowing already he knew what was in the envelope. Divorce papers, of course.

continued

While you let my analogy pool, chill a Collins glass, a tall, lean one with thinning hair. Pour gin, Campari and vermouth over ice in the glass shaker until it's a sun with commitment problems. Strain the Negroni over ice into the chilled glass, which suddenly seethes with a cold red fury.

Cracked Ice

When I return, I'll come in clapboard, stained
chestnut, with lead-based paint on radiators,
old-fashioned, and a little bit insane

but sturdy to a fault. A spalting grain
on punky myrtle and no refrigerator
when I return. I'll come in clapboard, stained

shake shingles skittering on skewed roof planes
that snarl the corner lot like unpaid panders,
old-fashioned and a little bitten, saying,

"Leave our sight lines sharp. Let dormers train
what angles water sheds." They congregate for
when I return. I'll come in clapboard, stained

You can be sure communication has broken down when your husband fails to mention he's divorcing you. Now we would be forced to interact, all the accusations spewing their psychotic orange.

with varnished truth: You ran me down. You caned
old rockers with prefab splints, hack renovator
refashioning me bit by bit, insane

to strip as spilth fine bulrush. I'll maintain
myself, then. There will be no mediators
when I return. I'll come in clapboard. Stained,
old-fashioned, I'll come a little bit insane.

The Negroni is ready for the twist—in my version, not of lemon, but of orange. An orange zest is long, gangly and not as easy to handle as a stubbier lemon, so you must concentrate. Position it over the glass when you twist it. I can't count how many bartenders I've seen who neglect this point. The hard wrench should yank the citric oil out of the peel and into the drink, where it lends a violent sarcasm to the proceedings that makes the truth easier to swallow. Twisting the peel also shapes it into an attractive spiral, although that is *not* your primary purpose, and an attractive spiral does *not* excuse denying a cocktail its lacerations. I've even seen some so-called barkeeps skip the twisting, instead gently *slipping* the zest into the glass, as if it were a tender thing not designed for abuse.

Do a Negroni a favor by extracting some spritz before you give up and drop that battered pip into its Technicolor grave.

Side Car. Grasshopper. King Cole. Mary Pickford. Sweet Jane. Glad Eyes. Gin Swizzle. Prairie Oyster. Southside. Halley's Comfort. Kiss Me Quick. Ruby Fizz. Coney Island Baby. Harry's Pick Me Up. Third Degree. Bronx Cocktail. Lime Rickey. Hot Toddy. Knockout. Belmont Stakes. Damn the Weather. Lady Be Good. Sloe Flip. Billy Taylor. Charlie Chaplin. Black Jack. Irish Fix. Planter's Punch. Clover Club. Tailspin. Buttergrog. Subway Cooler. Cold Deck. Special Rough. Special Rough. Special Rough.[19]

---

19. *Enter stage left: WEEKEND. The ARGUMENT will be begin at 7 p.m. Friday and continue until 8:30 a.m. Monday.*

    HUSBAND: (*Wondering aloud*) Why didn't you get any cantaloupe at King Kullen?

    WIFE: (*No answer*)

    HUSBAND: You should always get cantaloupe.

    WIFE: (*No answer*)

    HUSBAND: Hello?

    WIFE: What?

    HUSBAND: You should always pick up cantaloupe when you go to the store.

    WIFE: (*No answer*)

    HUSBAND: I'm talking to you.

    WIFE: I know you are.

    HUSBAND: So answer.

    WIFE: I wasn't aware you'd asked a question. I heard instead a demand. A demand for cantaloupe, to which my reply would go something like this: "I'm not your personal shopper. Get your own damn cantaloupe."

    > (*MARGUERITE looks up from playing on the kitchen floor. Begins BUZZING around like a bumble bee. She is NOT dancing with light sneakers.*)

    HUSBAND: It's simple. You go to the store, you pick up cantaloupe. Find your own place and

Whiskey Sour

Called in sick. Stayed home
sick. Could be the oysters,
that asshole behind the bar,

---

you can live off dark chocolate or whatever it is you eat, but while you're shopping for MY daughter in MY house, we're having fresh fruit.

> (*WIFE picks up APPLE from fruit bowl and tosses it at HUSBAND. HUSBAND, unflinching, watches it sail toward his chest, hit, rather merrily, and sink with a thunk onto the floor. MARGUERITE buzzes around the APPLE, circling it and flapping her wings. She lights on the apple—BZZZZT—and picks it up. She returns it to the fruit bowl.*)

HUSBAND: Oh great. That's a great example, throwing things in front of Marguerite. Good job, Mom.

WIFE: Please, I'm sure she doesn't recognize you since you're so rarely home.

HUSBAND: God, not that old refrain. I wake to sleep, and take my waking slow.

WIFE: There's nothing more to say.

HUSBAND: And always the tower, the boat, the distant train.

MARGUERITE: (I think I made you up inside my head.)

WIFE: Oh never try to knock on rotten wood.

APPLE: Rage, rage against the dying—   HUSBAND: She spent her money with such perfect style. WIFE: If I could tell you, I would let you know. HUSBAND: The art of losing isn't— WIFE: I learn by going where I have to—

MARGUERITE: Never try to know more than you should.

HUSBAND: Time can say nothing but I told you so.

WIFE: This melancholy moment will remain.

FRUIT BOWL: I couldn't help myself; I had to smile.

HUSBAND: I shut my eyes and all the world drops dead.

WIFE: Do not go gentle— WEEKEND: They are all gone away.

a glob of Tuesday's special
on Wednesday's fork,
par for a nonunion joint.

Could be getting dumped
over coffee. She never gets
coffee, I should have known.

Home sick. My blanket's
green, with linty bellflowers
in the unwashed grass. Last

night I drove through old maps.
A farm on this very spot.
The Battery walled against

the wilds. Green graves
and lovers. (Fields don't know
jack about the future.

The fate beneath them,
bedrock, foundations.)
Grass growing on Broadway,

imagine. Sheep grazing
the Bowery, spelled "Bowerie."
I drove through crooks

hanged, leaves on giant elms
in Washington Square.
This is all her fault. History

built on landfill. Paved.
Not like my blanket,
casual but tucked, a survivor.

How to Make a Brandy Stinger

To make a proper Brandy Stinger, you must imagine a future raked with broken
minesweepers, a series of trenches, fallback positions in a marriage still hoping to survive
its own fallout. The Brandy Stinger is what we accuse of our own failings. As I like to
craft it, it is rimmed in sugar, deceitful, coiled.

Before I mix the brandy with white crème de menthe, I make its beautiful, fatal habitat.
First, I rub a lime wedge along the edge of a martini glass, sliding it like a tongue over the
enamel tooth of a lie. The wet track my lime leaves is what the sugar will remember. I
aim for a ring of regular width, so that when I turn the glass upside down and dip the rim
into the plate of sugar, a perfect wedding-white band will crystallize. Then, in a shaker, I
measure two parts fire to one part liquid ice, dragonfly to stupid mistake. I chill, shake,
pour. Steady, now. There it goes, filling up to the widening lip.[20] It looks like
reconciliation, but the gesture is wearing thin.

---

20. He'll intrude on your field of vision in a blur of ravaged browns and steel-rimmed posture. *Don't
    cry*, he'll say. You will have fallen asleep sitting up, your mascara drying where it ran, an

continued

umbered face on the Eve of St. Crispin's Day. You will be prepared for a battle, but here he'll be, fervent and disarming. *It can't have been a mistake*, he will say. *A stupid mistake. Impossible. Think of our wedding night, the moon on the ocean, fire and bare feet dancing on the hard sand. Think of how we ran, laughter at the water's edge, past knots of friends, whispering spouses, kisses, to a private silvery spot where we hovered like dragonflies. Think of how you said, "This is better than I ever thought it could be."* He'll blaze eloquent, numbing you, distorting your more recent memories of cranberry juice like blood on the baby, leadbelly dinners, laundry detergent. For a moment, you will see his point of view: you will suppose, for argument's sake, you are those things he said before he left this evening:

- hysterical
- insane
- messy
- heedless
- sadistic
- perversely long-winded
- depressed
- detached
- distant
- condescending
- disruptive
- rude
- intolerant
- impatient
- prating
- irrational

Grading Rubrics for Children of Divorce

MECHANICS: Spelling, grammar and punctuation errors

"I like snaks," he wrote to filibuster
a blank school day, his cobras coiled back home
in a lunchbox. Six seemed much too young to master
the silent *e*, an extra chromosome

slithering like subtext at the ends
of sense, and who could fathom *–ght*?
There's *violins* and then there's *violence*,
two phone numbers, no bus some days, *say please*,

start at the top for *l, n, b* and *q*,
but *e* starts in the middle, twists on its spine,
gets trampled by horses, beggarly as Pew
in Chapter Five. "I hope he dies," my kind

- hostile
- meandering
- unsupportive
- teeth-sucking
- drawer-ajar-leaving
- hair-twirling
- unsexed
- cold

But then you must remember the Brandy Stinger, the poisonous cup which is never lifted to the lip
of its intended victim, which always goes to the Most Willing, which always goes to the Beloved.

boy hissed at story hour. He didn't know
he'd known so well that Pew would perish, a plot
point drawn like an *e* already in death throes
before the horses come, as afterthought.

We read, Pew died, he sobbed. "Mom, I like TV
where you don't care about the characters."
I put down *Treasure Island*. He asked "Where's
dead?" but meant another word, without the *e*.

STYLE: Little or no sentence fluency; many repetitions; incorrect vocabulary;
author does not communicate enthusiasm

For *rote*, read *rot*
For *dead*, read *dad*
For *knotty*, read *naughty*
For *Hades*, read *had*

For *The It* read *tithe*
For *heat* read *hate*
For *write* read *writhe*
For *meat* read *mate*

Desire is *reside*
Denude is *endure*
To seek is to hide
Fraction is *fracture*

ORGANIZATION: Introduction, body and conclusion do not follow format

Miss Deference scores a line: The principal
is Mr. Long but he isn't long, he's short.
No one's tuned to hear her hit the tact
nicely on the head. So unlike her,
said no one, as Greek gods bicker, social studies
of exclamation points. Under her desk
in wads of molded gum, her pencil pokes
the obverse of nipples or puts out Grecian eyes.
Is anyone under the radar under duress?
She's testing blunt-nosed scissors. When they cut
her arms, she'll starve and purge to get more edge,
less form. She's cleared for future vanishing points
where Ares and Harpina can howl Olympic
obscenities in zero relation to her.

CONTENT: Does not address the essay topic

What I'm trying to say is that when you divide
something in half, you divide it into two

equal parts, yes, and Dennis wants to share
his snacks equally with Sara. Draw a line

on each food to divide it in half, they said,
so I bisected the apple, the cheese cube, the pizza

slice, the ice cream cone with my fat black
crayon, but when they said, "Now color

each half differently," I could not do it. What
gods have joined, let no one put asunder.

Tips for Setting Up Your Own Bar

Material things are fun, but materialism is not.[21] In the world of wines, where single
bottles can sell at auctions for the kind of money single moms rarely see (the kind of

---

21. My soon-to-be ex was always transparently insecure about rich people, who are not nearly the
category he put them in. Some are boring with not enough tannin, some are loud and unworthy
but have mossy overtones, some are funny and great and the hint of cherry makes them
presentable for almost any occasion. And some, it's true, are highly specialized, tolerable only
with certain cheeses, say, or a particular kind of weather, and those will certainly complain if I try
to lug them along to a coffee hour, but so long as I remember *not* to lug them to coffee hours I'll
be fine and so will they. I encourage my daughter not to be cowed, but Lord knows, her "friends"
do their best to undermine me. Who are these Munich mannequins "in their sulphur loveliness,"
their kindergarten retinas already imprinted with various unaffordable logos?

   Her first day of school, a day much heralded by various readings and rereadings of picture
books about kindergarten, Marguerite displayed her characteristic caution, marching forth with
shoulders squared, her generic pale green backpack a half-hardened tortoiseshell. She
emerged a few fraught hours later, her wariness intact. "Mommy," she confided, "this isn't a real
school. It's fake. All we do is play."

   The next day she emerged disconsolate, not because of the play, but because her backpack
had become a source of derision for failing to bear the Hello Kitty® trademark ($32.00–

money that would cover a year's tuition at a very good school, the kind of money he ought to invest willingly in her education), materialism becomes hopelessly expensive and un-fun almost at once. Stock your cabinet with a few offbeat wines that will charm the affluent but not compete with them. Bull's Blood, for example, is the vintner's equivalent of slumming: exotic, cheap, clever and authentic in the way rich people love. Plus it really does taste almost like blood. Pair it with fresh kill or salted wound.

And to appear ironic instead of poor, Tickled Pink, brought to you by Boone's Farm, is the best option. It's carbonated with a chipper strawberry flavor that's hilarious for a minute and then sickening. I suppose it was meant to approximate pink champagne, but the execution of the concept in the instance of Tickled Pink is more Kool-Aid than cuvée. For sheer camp, it's unbeatable.[22]

$125.00, "Help your student bring her schoolbooks home in royal princess style"). I smelled a Learning Opportunity, as Miss Burns, her kindergarten teacher, might say: we discussed feudalism, mostly from the serf's point of view, and I steered her toward the hopeful conclusion that, in our country, we can all be princesses if we use our imaginations and work hard in school. Then we stopped at the craft store for sequins ($3.98), rhinestones ($4.98) and fabric paint ($6.73, "Value 6-packs with the most popular colors are available in Glitter, Shiny, and Iridescent") and returned home to lard her backpack with "royal princess style."

   The third day, fearing yet more ridicule, she refused to wear it, though I insisted. "You'll see," I promised, loading up her snack bag with corn muffin and carrots. Marguerite looked stricken. That day her father picked her up after school and presented her with a brand new Hello Kitty backpack. "Top-of-the-line," he said. "Only the best for my princess."

22. Which is why, after he'd served divorce papers, broken his leg, worn a hip cast for six months, went on an extended business trip involving film production companies and reissues of eighties dance songs that were "big in France," and finally, finally signed a separation agreement, I felt

continued

entitled to a night out of my own, and why, upon discovering I had less than five dollars to blow on a thoughtful gift for the host, I swung by Second Avenue and picked up some Tickled Pink.

The party was at a restaurant I'd never have thought of entering because it had the word "Ye" in its name. I raised the Tickled Pink up to the neon sign in a dry toast and dove in. It was the best party I've ever attended. Everyone made me laugh. By that I don't mean I was sneering at them. I mean that every guest in this restaurant was a funny person by nature, and played their good humor at full volume, and insisted on visiting me with it, even though I barely knew anyone there. My job at this party was simply to stay put while others laid their golden observations, wit, stories, improbabilities, bits, timings and jokes at my feet as if I were the baby Jesus in the Christmas pageant and they were the heavenly hosts.

One in particular stood out. Well, his hair stood out, literally, in fetching, aristocratic, leonine waves, but with a cowlick at the front that you could tell he'd worked on relentlessly, to no avail. No volume of gel, spray, spritz or goop was going to persuade that yank of hair to stand up with the rest. It insisted on curling its way down over his forehead, leaving a kind of lopsided mass of other, more upright lions to rule over the crown. His eyes were gold. He was a writer. It was all too much. A literary lion.

We circled, smitten. Feint. Jab. Cover up. Clinch. Standing 8 Count. Two outfighters in their crouches. I was a tomato can, I thought. Palooka. He was the professional. Or the Marquess, watching, directing me to punch out of the bear hug or surrender. Our eyes in lockdown. Ye Olde place had become crowded and suddenly we were mashed, our feet off the ground, a swell of bodies pushing us together in a sweet science of full body contact, as if, as if, as if. After three years out of the ring, my training gone to rack, my insides padded to indifference, the spring and ripple, the tensed drum of a man's skin against mine felt like some glorious brain injury I'd never regret. The crush carried us, chest to chest, his cocktail still in his hand. Blithe.

"Did you order this?"

"Why, yes."

He put his glass to my lips and I sipped the only calm taste in a wrestle of massed people. A Millionaire. Bourbon, Pernod, triple sec, grenadine. For a moment, the press eased. We fell back until my feet touched carpet, but only for a pause, because then the crowd surged, lunged, and whatever wave engulfed the writer and me channeled itself into the Ladies' Room,

Hot Little Cricket Sonnet that Wants Wants Wants

but hasn't, being all but sex, all filch, iambic
shanked and muscle mad to batten

him thigh to knee but leave an oxygen
enough for one keen lust to breathe and want

---

where we broke like rollers on the vanity counter just as the boy in the punk hairdo next to me vomited. Bells. The blunt rabbit-punch stench of spit-up. The muted whine of voices, like the plane going down and nothing but Andes. Somewhere some dam broke, beings found their space again, and immediately the sorting out began, the Hell to Pay, the fines for violation of fire code and simple dust-off recovery. I was back on my feet and so was Lion and just then would have been the moment for the roundhouse, the haymaker, the wild swing to the lip, the kiss, fool, kiss, but we were on our feet now, barf was in my hair, on my face, all over my clothes, I blinked, Lion fled, and then so did I.

Ye Olde paper towels, Ye Olde hot water spigot welded shut, Ye Olde weave your way, orderly and silent, back out to an alley. Ye Olde party over. And there he was, right in front of me, bending over to pick vomit out of the tread of his hightops with a small, uncooperative twig. I found myself wavering at the ropes, then I stepped in.

"Hey," I said.

"Hey," he said.

"Hey," I said again, then, gathering one of those June-time, first-bout fistfuls of air, continued gamely, "I have a burning question."

"Fire away," he said. He was clever like that.

I exhaled. "If I had kissed you in the Ladies' Lounge, would you have kissed me back?"

He looked at me with the same mask of incredulity he'd worn when the guy vomited on us. "Yes," he said slowly, appraisingly, as if about to make a purchase of a slightly chipped but still valuable antique lamp. "Yes," without blinking, "I think I would have."

but want what crickets want, fair hearing played
at night: he lie, he lay, he lain, he lay,

he laid me on the salt and pepper hay,
he weltered, yarrow, fey as lemonade

or something like that beyond the crunk of kenning,
like saxifrage, Stonehenge, like fibulae

to ideate my chamber, not dactyls but forewings
trussed by joints and rhyme up-roughening,

all tug and ballast, sinkhole, clubfoot weighed,
not worded: but touch me I will turn to thing.

How to Make a Piña Colada

A blender drink is family, cells and DNA strands and compatible kidneys and one
marrow that's the spitting image of another's. How do you turn from what is so much a
part of you, especially when you're churned into one indistinguishable smoothie?
Coladas can muster no distinction, only the fact of their viscid coldness. I sling rum,
pineapple juice and coconut cream in a blender filled with ice and let it rip. My mother
always said don't stick anything metal in the blender while it's running, but you know
how it is. The place is busy, the service bar is backed up, a guy behind this colada crew is
waiting to order and one of the waiters keeps singing the opening bars of "Do You
Know the Way to San Jose" over and over, like a toddler asking why. I nudge the ice
with the stirrer while the blades fume until that funnel appears, smooth and symmetrical,

the physics of centrifugal force solving the mystery of solids. I'll pour it into a parfait
glass, something pretty, and flag it.

(Tropical Drink Garnish

Vermin eyes set close and mean, face drawn tight,
fear spreading across it like mange, fear inculcated by bigger
rats who've already fled, he's cornered, yes, surrounded by flags,

hawed, rather, hemmed in—*a bad deal*—hamstrung
by caution's rubber hopples: *There is no doubt in my mind*,
he says. *Spooky.* Always the adult impersonator, he'll try

backslapping to freedom. *Don't tell 'em your price, heh, heh.*
He pokes the attorney general with his elbow.
O to snap the tension of a cogitabund frowny face

as if it were a training bra on the most popular girl
and then make a run for it. Liberty, piñatas, Hamm's Beer,
now *those* were the days, hey! like that shindig in Maine,

the Cutty Sark sliding through troubled conversational waters
with gale-proof—*Now, she was a looker*—congeniality,
though what with the wonks, donors and spinners floating around,

a fella could hardly get a crack in edgewise, plus you had to be careful
what you said. He thought he'd been doing pretty darn good
in the charm department, until he saw that PR lady

in the red suit mouth to her pal, *He's drunk,* as if she knew
how drunk hung on him, as if she had a key to his walk-in closet,
for chrissake—I mean, there's *image,* and then there's the soul

inside the image: this is a spiritualistic man. *And what,
Mr. President, do you talk about with your dad when you're not
talking politics? Pussy.* But our ex-President's on the lam

while this poem so uselessly muses, he's breaking out, fleet as an undisclosed
location, the poor man's being run ruthlessly down.
Secret Servicemen named Cutty and Sark are gaining ground,

while whispering delicately into their electronical whirligigs,
and just as they leap to tackle him, he transforms, Mylar
and crepe and dainty toothpick toes so only Kennebunk-pink

flesh tones linger in the ornamental hues of the parasol's bloom,
its ribs radially attached, functional as a Big Person's umbrella,
and praying to stay dry: once wet, it bleeds cheap dye.)

A colada seems bland and harmless, except for the coconut cream, which keeps forever,
always a worrisome trait. And what other than coconut is in that skinny can? Why is there
so much fine print on its label? And why is the can always almost empty? I make a note
("More life!") in the bar book tucked next to the register or behind the Galliano or in that
little space between the ice bin and the bar, any good spot for not forgetting something
you won't refer to much. Out of the way, but not too.

It's getting late. Red's on the other side of the bar, telling an old-timer about the time he worked on a Portuguese fishing vessel and watched a grown man weep at mackerel. We're wrecked, the second-to-last customer shipped out long ago, the place is deserted, even the waiters have gone. But it's not yet closing time. To throw that guy out now and go to bed would be to admit something terrible, a drifting from the landfall of work, of using time well. Sleep is for dead people, the unoccupied.

Sometimes shifts have second winds. If we can keep a last customer going long enough, we'll hit the pay dirt of after-hours, when bartenders and waitstaff from other establishments congregate for their own private and spontaneous shot of camaraderie. Good tippers, all, they're bad for the house—sympathy runs much too fast for running tabs to keep up—but very fulfilling for the tip cup, and fun in a war-torn kind of way. Welcome to after-hours, liberty in a defensive crouch logging itself like the 86'd customers in the spiral notebook, a Bic pen permanently stuck in its mangled wire binding. Knots of blue yarn, epaulets on a dead soldier.

I can't yet shake the knack of waiting,[23] blaming myself for my empty shift. I don't yet want to. Let's fix ourselves a Rusty Nail, too. Rusty Nails go on the rocks: there's simply no other way to serve up revenge, which tastes dilutedly sweet, although the Rusty Nail is one hundred percent liquor. I always chill the glass. A cold vessel takes a little of the hard edge off this surprisingly potent elixir. No garnish, of course. Just five fingers, scotch and Drambuie, wrapped around those rocks.

---

23. Waiting on him.

Rusty Nails would be desperate and bleak were it not for Drambuie. Drambuie, interestingly,[24] is one of those curiosities that can never be satisfactorily explained, like grace, or what investment bankers do, or codependence. It is classified as a liqueur, although beyond that impassive revelation we tread at our peril. The recipe is secret; we know only that Drambuie is cobbled together either from scotch itself or from whatever is left after making scotch, and from herbs unknown, and from honey. The final touch is honey. And not just honey, heather honey, in which even the honeycomb and the honeybees are boiled down—oh those Celts! How they suffer! How those around them suffer! All those glorious, unsuspecting bees, consumed like one's own children might be in a myth.

Also, interestingly, Drambuie was brought to us not by clever, bored clergy, as was Chartreuse or Benedictine, but by a clan of Scots, the Mackinon family.[25] The Gaelic word *drambuie* translates to Drink of Satisfaction. I've been known to indulge in a Rusty Nail myself, to savor the self-inflicted wounds as the golden hour melts to nectar.

Mead

Heather, heath, yield no flower to the *uisce beatha*,
D'eau de vie, de apple brandy, give no grape, no barley

mash, none o' that, fan-fan, fanned by wings of bees
I sent you once. You've spread again, chicory, your knees

---

24. Not to him, who never asked me anything, to whom idle questions were corrosion in the tempered steel monologue he called communication, but to me, interestingly, and perhaps to you.

25. Scottish clans are known for their centuries-long internecine vendettas. My, it is late.

too like Appalachians worn aslope, your valley's
crotch too crocheted with ling for colonies

to collapse forever. Once smarmy in nectar, Royal Jelly
bean-sized sharps and lazers swarmed here, vinegar Crosbys

crooned. Now no honey to be had, but fogg and lees, fogg and lees
in the vale where jab and smother atrophied.

It's a Dark Age after being lit upon. Though lonely, be not free
in your abandon for no better reasons than these:

Husbandry cannot be mneme for honeybees.
Were I with you I'd foment ferment fervently

Home Brews

Did you know that you can make mead in your own kitchen, just like the Picts might
have back in 200 B.C., simply by fermenting honey? A jar or two in a high cabinet, for old
times' sake. According to Pliny the Elder, you need only rainwater, honey and five years.
"Some who are more expert," he writes, "use rain-water as soon as it has fallen, boiling it
down to a third of the quantity and adding one part of old honey to three parts of water,
and then keeping the mixture in the sun for 40 days after the rising of the Dog-star"
(p. 445, *Sacred and Herbal Healing Beers*). Then they wait five years. Everybody waits, even
the experts, even Pliny, who's already quite elderly.

If you try this at home, make sure you remember that *while* is the operative word. Otherwise, you're not waiting, you're lying in wait, like a hunter, a tarantula, not the gatherer you are. Go make something of those five years that's not a revenge fantasy.[26] Besides, once it meets Petrunkevitch's digger wasp, we can't say the tarantula's lying-in-wait strategy works very well, just as we can't say with any authority that the Picts made mead. For God's sake, all they left were a few carvings and one list of kings, everything else, destroyed.[27]

Here's what we can say about mead: no matter how fertile destruction may be, yeast breaking down sugar, revenge has nothing to do with it. Nothing sweet or moral is born

---

26. You see, I'd read a recipe for revenge, a simple one calling for half-eaten shrimp and curtain rods and an agreement to leave the apartment for a reasonably large sum. On my hypothetical last night, I would collect the check, send Marguerite to a Monster Playdate, pack, treat myself to shrimp and caviar and, lastly, insert one half-eaten, caviar-dipped shrimp tail into every curtain rod in the place, replacing the cap with gingerly love. Then I'd leave. And wait for the stench to overpower my ex, my ex's friends, my ex's potential new lover, my ex's peace of mind, my ex's so-called charms, my ex's way with kids, my ex's attorney, his army of exterminators and Real Estate Professionals, my ex's sense of superiority. Nine months later, with no labor, not having broken a sweat, I would call, claiming to miss the ole homestead, and, thinking *She has no idea what a raw deal she's getting, heh heh*, he'd sell it back to me at a tenth of the price. Then I would unpack, remove the shrimp tails from the curtain rods, open the windows, and live happily ever after.

27. Oh, to write a handbook for my child's fair pain. She has to build on the ruins of a warrior civilization, one that a few scholars and I believe had a matriarchic strain, based on various carvings of mirrors and combs. She must make, not make *for*, not make *up*, to be a child of the universe instead of her broken family.

out of revenge. Also, we should let nature take its course—digger wasps will be digger wasps—but if yours is to serve who only stand and wait, fight it.

FAQs About Extreme Unction

The idea is to get the forgiving done before you have an actual corpse, but only if you will have an actual corpse.[28] Anoint the five senses— eyes, ears, nostrils, lips, hands—and, in the case of men only, the loins. Anointing a woman's loins is strictly forbidden. Perhaps hers are in no need of forgiving. Perhaps hers are too icky for the priest to handle. The question of loins is only one of many angels-on-a-pinhead type debates about Extreme Unction. Here are a few more:

How close to death do you have to be to qualify?
You MUST be about to croak, though certain California nuns would dispute us. If you're not really in mortal danger, God will never forgive your impudence, just as He will never forgive California.

---

28. Divorce serves the same idea. It anoints the death of a family in notarized date stamps that smell guilty precisely because they lead inexorably to that death. The rite is a little different, involving Partial Stipulations So Ordered, a Plaintiff, hereinafter referred to as the "Husband" and "Father," the word *Whereas* repeated many times, and plenty of Xeroxing. But the idea's the same, and so is the flaw in the idea, since in both cases the process of exculpation looks, sounds, tastes, smells and feels more like a process of execution. And both raise suspicions of inefficacy. Does a dab of oil at the second-to-last breath really rub out sin? And when the judge signs the true copy duly entered and the divorce is GRANTED, has he any power to give, much less forgive? Children know better: you can't forgive someone who's not dead yet. Research

continued

Must baptized infants on the verge of death be denied Extreme Unction?
Yes, though they can be confirmed. If you are a baptized infant on the verge of death, ask for the sacrament of Confirmation instead.

Is Extreme Unction really a sacrament or just a nice, vaguely holy thing to do?
It's really a sacrament no it's not yes it is is not is too I'm telling Mom, she bit me

If you use the indicative "I anoint thee . . ." instead of a prayer form, does it count?
Nope, sorry.

The excess of debate, together with the taboo on women's pubic area, makes me leery, as if it were all an elaborate cover, a rationalization, as if the priest were the shooter, the rites of forgiveness a masque for the benefit of the conferrer, not the dying body. It can't be pure accident that the word *unction* has come to mean "exaggerated, assumed, or superficial earnestness of language or manner" (*Webster's*).

For an impromptu self-administered dose of extreme unction in that latter sense, read the portentous bullshit on the label of a Jägermeister bottle, claiming to be a poem by Otto von Riesenthal written in 1848:

> *Das ist des Jägers Ehrenschild,*
> *daß er beschützt und hegt sein Wild,*

---

bears out that children of dead people adapt to the loss of a parent more quickly and effectively than children of divorced people, who remain unresolved the rest of their lives. The news isn't all bad, though. Children of divorce are better than average at detecting unctuousness.

weidmännisch jagt, wie sich's gehört,
den Schöpfer im Geschöpfe ehrt.

In English, please:

This is the hunter's badge of honour,
    that he protect and nourish his game,
    hunt sportingly, as is proper,
    and honour the Creator in creation.[29]

Would that be before or after he kills it?

---

29. This is the sort of rationalization my ex favored. "It wounds me to have to say this," he'd begin, before sinking the knife into my anterior lobe. Why not "I hate you," or "I want you dead"? The conventional wisdom in divorce books is to never say anything bad about your ex-spouse. It's unfair to your children, who love the bastard. On the other hand, the greatest responsibility of a parent, one that Otto von Riesenthal has clearly shirked, is to pass on a coherent worldview. How do I explain coherently why I am no longer married to Marguerite's father without saying anything bad about him? In my worldview, he represents blind aggressiveness, the tendency to hunt sportingly that which is not game: me.

    I quit tending bar. I keep books now, balancing sheets, toting up assets and liabilities, working alone at home, and open the door only to Marguerite, who knows the secret knock.

A sure sign someone drinks too much is when he decides that beer and wine don't count as alcohol and therefore he can have as much of them as he wants. Now, the fact that he's counting his drinks at all is bad enough; if he feels compelled to leave some out, he's downright lost. Moreover, it's not true that beer and wine don't count, and even if they didn't, a person can lose himself to anything, anyone, anywhere, practically without thinking, just by saying *yes* or *I do.*[30]

Lots of Europeans drink their beer at room temperature. Only here do we feel the need to refrigerate everything, even radishes, at the expense of their bite. When I pour a beer, one

---

30. The reckoning:

Assets	Liabilities
Briefing Room, June 17, 2009, Remarks by the President: . . . historic economic crisis . . . cascade of mistakes . . . regulatory structures to prevent abuse . . . twenty-first-century global economy . . . easy money . . . schemes . . . pile of sand . . . off guard . . . responsibility . . . responsibility . . . responsibility . . . lasting foundation for prosperity.	I've learned nothing except that to know Thyself is not as useful as knowing the Other. Pennyroyal rids the body of vermin. Brooklime drives out crudities.
Sanitation procedures for Department of Defense: Conduct security review and physically remove information with an X-Acto-style razor knife or scissors.	My dangers are not so retractable. For example, we scissored the pear into perfect halves. I ate mine, but it wasn't enough.
History. We are not doomed to repeat it because we've forgotten. We merely disliked the outcome and seek another.	*Anyone suffering from gripes and sand should abjure pears altogether.*

that's not chilled to the point of brittleness, I tilt the glass, let the amber slide down its slope, and think about two child legs swinging from a tree, just out of reach. [31]

Assets	Liabilities
U.S. troops killed in Iraq since the invasion: 4,314. Iraqi civilians killed since the invasion: We don't do body counts but definitely more.	You don't have to practice being poor or dead. You'll figure it out when the time comes.
In Job 38:1–11 we find God's sense of humor on display. It's bitter, but we're gladdened to know He has one.	*The seeds of throughwax ground to a powder and added in pea-size doses to the porridge of young children will heal ruptures.*
Our Nuclear Family: Mother, Father, China, France, India, Israel, North Korea, Pakistan, South Africa.	Progeny, from L. "begotten," not made: I do Marguerite the mercy of aspiring to the passive.
We the People, in order to form a more perfect union.	*The moss that grows on small trees possesses a drying, astringent power and faculty.*

The balance must be zero. The only sane answer is nothing.

31. My first-ever true love grew up to be a brewmaster. He had a lean build, a good arm and a survivalist's quietude. When she was angry at him, which was often, his mother would call him by his first and middle name, emphasis on the otherwise untapped middle. "John Da-VID!" she'd rap out, and I would freeze in fear that my rabbinically wise, tan, lithe, skillful, uncommunicative protector would be whisked away to some cellar. I was four, already worried about preservation. Already building that misguided long view.

Jägermeister, Double Shot

I used to be hot, but now

        I keep an eye on Estonia from time to time

there's too much gravity, a sag

        and other areas of relative entropy

        and also relative peace

a flatland, underground stream. rubble

        from mountaintop removal or such ozone depletions

        as

scars the cheekbone. If only you had died, not

        polluted the discourse, brought discord to

        the ringing spheres

     our small talk, twinkling

        out there in outer beltways where Pluto yet orbits,

        disinherited space junk

keeping a cold eye on the bodies of the solar system

On Pouring a Good Stout

Time is the main ingredient. A thirst cannot truly be quenched without it. For stout, the measure is in the pour. There's no rush, but slowness is by and large misunderstood, and so rushing remains the norm. For instance, right now I'm at one of those blood drives which constitute the extent of my service impulse these days. I am watching my blood seep into a sterilized plastic bag while my daughter—our daughter—reads *King of the Wind* by Marguerite Henry (illustrated by Wesley Dennis, Rand McNally & Co., Chicago, ©1948) with such intensity she can't hear me call out to her to stop twirling her hair. Your own blood in quantity is darker than you think it should be, and the color and stealth with which it accumulates remind me of pouring a stout, which ends up dark, but which foams from the tap into the glass a rich, wild tan, like "a clear bay—whose coat is touched with gold. When he flees under the sun he is the wind" (p. 53). That's the first color: steed-tan. And active, with tiny bubbles parading up and down in columns, particles swirling and tossing their manes, hooves tearing at silky hide. I fill the pint glass a third of the way and let it sit for a good five minutes, until all the animals have settled down, the bay has floated to the top and thickened, leaving the blood brooding below. And I pour another third, and the horses start and whinny. And I wait, patient, wise, silent, wiry, like my brewmaster love ("The only 'uman bein' what can 'andle 'im is a spindlin' boy," p. 107) until all is calm again. And I pour the last third, and the thick head rises up, up past the rim of the pint, but it doesn't spill because I have been patient and slow and wise. It stays put, my prayer, my possession, not quite broken, reading in her chair.

Sources

"Mickey Mouse Media," by Eric Alterman, *The Nation*, May 19, 2008.

The New York Bartender's Guide, edited by Sally Ann Berk, Black Dog & Leventhal, New York, ©1994.

Sacred and Herbal Healing Beers, by Stephen Harrod Buhner, Siris Books, Boulder, Colo., ©1998.

The Book of Common Prayer, Church Publishing, New York, 1979.

The Craft of the Cocktail, by Dale DeGroff, Clarkson Potter, New York, ©2002.

King of the Wind: The Story of the Godolphin Arabian, by Marguerite Henry, illustrated by Wesley Dennis, Rand McNally & Co., Chicago, ©1948.

The Art of the Bar, by Jeff Hollinger and Rob Schwartz, Chronicle Books, San Francisco, ©2006.

Alexis Lichine's New Encyclopedia of Wines & Spirits, by Alexis Lichine, Knopf, New York, ©1967.

"6+1 Trait Writing Continuum," Northwest Regional Educational Laboratory, Portland, Oreg., ©2007.

Oxford American Dictionary, edited by Eugene Ehrlich et al., Oxford University Press, New York, ©1980.

The Oxford Universal Dictionary, Oxford University Press, London, ©1955.

Sauer's Herbal Cures, translated and edited by William Woys Weaver, Routledge, New York, ©2001.

Counterinsurgency, by David Petraeus, Department of Defense, U.S. Army, final draft, June 2006.

"Prodigal Son," by Jake Tapper, http://www.salon.com/news/feature/1994/04/09/bush/index1.html, cites David Fink of the *Hartford Courant* speaking with George Bush at the 1988 Republican National Convention, New Orleans, La., Aug. 14, 1988.

Walden and Other Writings, by Henry David Thoreau, Modern Library, New York, ©2000.

Mr. Boston: Official Bartender's and Party Guide, Warner Books, New York, ©1994.

Webster's New International Dictionary, 2nd edition, unabridged, G. & C. Merriam Co., Springfield, Mass., ©1951.

Webster's Ninth New Collegiate Dictionary, Merriam-Webster, Springfield, Mass., ©1985,

The villanelle refrains in footnote 19 are from the following poems:

W. H. Auden, "Villanelle"; Elizabeth Bishop, "One Art"; Tom Disch, "The Rapist's Villanelle"; Sylvia Plath, "Admonitions" and "Solipsism (Mad Girl's Love Song)"; Edwin Arlington Robinson, "The House on the Hill"; Theodore Roethke, "The Waking"; Mark Strand, "Two de Chiricos"; and Dylan Thomas, "Do Not Go Gentle into That Good Night." Sylvia Plath's poems "Balloons" and "The Munich Mannequins" are quoted in other footnotes. The italicized portions in footnote 30 are from *Sauer's Herbal Cures*, by Christopher Sauer, pp. 350 and 216.

Acknowledgments

Some of the poems and prose in *Bar Book* first appeared in these magazines:

Barrow Street: "How to Make a Martini"

Drunken Boat: "Jägermeister, Double Shot" and "Malted Barley"

filling Station: "Hot Little Cricket Sonnet that Wants Wants Wants"

The Journal: "Solar Plexus"

Notre Dame Review: "Warning Label on Bottle of Boodles," "Tom Collins," "How to Make an Old Fashioned," Interior Life of Tumbler," "How to Cure a Hangover" and "Fernet-Branca"

Parnassus: "Grading Rubrics for Children of Divorce"

Prairie Schooner: "Rusty Nail," "Pink Lady," "Old Fashioned" and "Brandy Stinger"

Raritan: "Here Are Lions," "Steaming Bull," "Obsolete Cocktails" and "Sea Breeze"

The Southampton Review: How to Make a Mudslide," "Tickled Pink," "How to Make a Pink Lady," "Interruption by Singapore Sling," "How to Make a Shirley Temple" and "Shirley Temple"

Southwest Review: "Cracked Ice" under the title "Big Crazy Victorian"

Yale Review: "Field Manual for Counterinsurgency at Paul's Lounge"